AUDUBON GUIDE
to the National Wildlife Refuges

New England

AUDUBON GUIDE
to the National Wildlife Refuges

New England

Connecticut · Maine · Massachusetts
New Hampshire · Rhode Island · Vermont

By René Laubach

Foreword by Theodore Roosevelt IV

Series Editor, David Emblidge
Editor, Donald Young

A Balliett & Fitzgerald Book
St. Martin's Griffin, New York

Cartography: © Balliett & Fitzgerald, Inc. produced by Mapping Specialists Ltd.
Illustrations: Mary Sundstrom
Cover design: Michael Storrings and Sue Canavan
Interior design: Bill Cooke and Sue Canavan

Balliett & Fitzgerald Inc. Staff
Sue Canavan, Design Director
Maria Fernandez, Production Editor
Alexis Lipsitz, Executive Series Editor
Rachel Deutsch, Associate Photo Editor
Kristen Couse, Associate Editor
Paul Paddock, Carol Petino Assistant Editors
Howard Klein, Editorial Intern
Scott Prentzas and Diane Amussen, Copy Editors

Balliett & Fitzgerald Inc. would like to thank the following people for their
assistance in creating this series:
At National Audubon Society:
    Katherine Santone, former Director of Publishing, for sponsoring this project
    Claire Tully, Senior Vice President, Marketing
    Evan Hirsche, Director, National Wildlife Refuges Campaign
At U.S. Fish & Wildlife Service:
    Richard Coleman, Chief, Division of Refuges, U.S. Fish & Wildlife Service
    Janet Tennyson, Outreach Coordinator
    Craig Rieben, Chief of Broadcasting & Audio Visual, U.S. Fish & Wildlife
        Service, for photo research assistance
    Pat Carrol, Chief Surveyor, U.S. Fish & Wildlife Service, for map information
    Regional External Affairs officers, at the seven U.S. Fish & Wildlife Service
        Regional Headquarters
    Elizabeth Jackson, Photographic Information Specialist, National
        Conservation Training Center, for photo research
At St. Martin's Griffin:
    Greg Cohn, who pulled it all together on his end, as well as Michael
        Storrings and Kristen Macnamara
At David Emblidge—Book Producer:
    Marcy Ross, Assistant Editor
Thanks also to Theodore Roosevelt IV and John Flicker.

CONTENTS

VERMONT

Missisquoi NWR **135**
Swanton

Appendix

Foreword

America is singularly blessed in the amount and quality of land that the federal government holds in trust for its citizens. No other country can begin to match the variety of lands in our national wildlife refuges, parks and forests. From the Arctic Refuge on the North Slope of Alaska to the National Key Deer Refuge in Florida, the diversity of land in the National Wildlife Refuge (NWR) System is staggering.

Yet of all our public lands, the National Wildlife Refuge System is the least well known and does not have an established voting constituency like that of the Parks System. In part this is because of its "wildlife first" mission, which addresses the needs of wildlife species before those of people. That notwithstanding, wildlife refuges also offer remarkable opportunities for people to experience and learn about wildlife—and to have fun doing so!

The Refuge System was launched in 1903 when President Theodore Roosevelt discovered that snowy egrets and other birds were being hunted to the brink of extinction for plumes to decorate ladies' hats. He asked a colleague if there were any laws preventing the president from making a federal bird reservation out of an island in Florida's Indian River. Learning there was not, Roosevelt responded, "Very well, then I so declare it." Thus Pelican Island became the nation's first plot of land to be set aside for the protection of wildlife. Roosevelt went on to create another 50 refuges, and today there are more than 500 refuges encompassing almost 93 million acres, managed by the U.S. Fish & Wildlife Service.

The Refuge System provides critical habitat for literally thousands of mammals, birds, amphibians and reptiles, and countless varieties of plants and flowers. More than 55 refuges have been created specifically to save endangered species. Approximately 20 percent of all threatened and endangered species in the United States rely on these vital places for their survival. As a protector of our country's natural diversity, the System is unparalleled.

Setting NWR boundaries is determined, as often as possible, by the needs of species that depend on the protected lands. Conservation biology, the science that studies ecosystems as a whole, teaches us that wildlife areas must be linked by habitat "corridors" or run the risk of becoming biological islands. The resulting inability of species to transfer their genes over a wide area leaves them vulnerable to disease and natural disasters. For example, the Florida panther that lives in Big Cypress Swamp suffers from a skin fungus, a consequence, scientists believe, of inbreeding. Today's refuge managers are acutely aware of this precarious situation afflicting many species and have made protection of the System's biodiversity an important goal.

Clearly, the job of the refuge manager is not an easy one. Chronic underfunding of the System by the federal government has resulted in refuges operating with less money per employee and per acre than any other federal land-management agency. Recent efforts by some in Congress to address this shortfall have begun to show results, but the System's continued vulnerability to special interests has resulted in attempts to open refuges to oil drilling, road building in refuge wilderness areas, and military exercises.

The managers of the System have played a crucial role in responding to the limited resources available. They have created a network of volunteers who contribute tens of thousands of hours to help offset the lack of direct financing for the Refuge System. Groups like refuge "friends" and Audubon Refuge Keepers have answered the call for local citizen involvement on many refuges across the country.

I hope Americans like yourself who visit our national wildlife refuges will come away convinced of their importance, not only to wildlife but also to people. I further hope you will make your views known to Congress, becoming the voice and voting constituency the Refuge System so desperately needs.

—*Theodore Roosevelt IV*

Preface

Thank you for adding the *Audubon Guide to the National Wildlife Refuge System* to your travel library. I hope you will find this nine-volume series an indispensable guide to finding your way around the refuge system, as well as a valuable educational tool for learning more about the vital role wildlife refuges play in protecting our country's natural heritage.

It was nearly 100 years ago that Frank Chapman, an influential ornithologist, naturalist, publisher and noted Audubon member, approached President Theodore Roosevelt (as recounted by Theodore Roosevelt IV in his foreword), eventually helping to persuade him to set aside more than 50 valuable parcels of land for the protection of wildlife.

Because of limited funding available to support these new wildlife sanctuaries, Audubon stepped up and paid for wardens who diligently looked after them. And so began a century of collaboration between Audubon and the National Wildlife Refuge System. Today, Audubon chapter members can be found across the country assisting refuges with a range of projects, from viewing tower construction to bird banding.

Most recently, National Audubon renewed its commitment to the Refuge System by launching a nationwide campaign to build support for refuges locally and nationally. Audubon's Wildlife Refuge Campaign is promoting the Refuge System through on-the-ground programs such as Audubon Refuge Keepers (ARK), which builds local support groups for refuges, and Earth Stewards, a collaboration with the U.S. Fish and Wildlife Service and the National Fish and Wildlife Foundation, which uses refuges and other important bird habitats as outdoor classrooms. In addition, we are countering legislative threats to refuges in Washington, D.C., while supporting increased federal funding for this, the least funded of all federal land systems.

By teaching more people about the important role refuges play in conserving our nation's diversity of species—be they birds, mammals, amphibians, reptiles, or plants—we have an opportunity to protect for future generations our only federal lands system set aside first and fore-most for wildlife conservation.

As a nation, we are at a critical juncture—do we continue to sacrifice wetlands, forests, deserts, and coastal habitat for short-term profit, or do we accept that the survival of our species is closely linked to the survival of others? The National Wildlife Refuge System is a cornerstone of America's conservation efforts. If we are to leave a lasting legacy and, indeed, ensure our future, then we must build on President Theodore Roosevelt's greatest legacy. I invite you to join us!

—*John Flicker, President, National Audubon Society*

Introduction
to the National Wildlife Refuge System

He spent entire days on horseback, traversing the landscape of domed and crumbling hills, steep forested coulees, with undulating tables of prairie above. The soft wraparound light of sunset displayed every strange contour of the Badlands and lit the colors in each desiccated layer of rock—yellow, ochre, beige, gold.

Theodore Roosevelt was an easterner. As some well-heeled easterners were wont to do, he traveled west in 1883 to play cowboy, and for the next eight years he returned as often as possible. He bought a cattle ranch, carried a rifle and a six-gun, rode a horse. North Dakota was still Dakota Territory then, but the Plains bison were about gone, down to a scattering of wild herds.

The nation faced a new and uneasy awareness of limits during Roosevelt's North Dakota years. Between 1776 and 1850, the American population had increased from 1.5 million to more than 23 million. National borders were fixed and rail and telegraph lines linked the coasts, but Manifest Destiny had a price. The ongoing plunder of wildlife threatened species such as the brown pelican and the great egret; the near-total extermination of 60 million bison loomed as a lesson many wished to avoid repeating.

Despite the damage done, the powerful landscapes of the New World had shaped the outlooks of many new Americans. From Colonial-era botanist John Bartram to 19th-century artists George Catlin and John James Audubon, naturalists and individuals of conscience explored the question of what constituted a proper human response to nature. Two figures especially, Henry David Thoreau and John Muir, created the language and ideas that would confront enduring Old World notions of nature as an oppositional, malevolent force to be harnessed and exploited. The creation in 1872 of Yellowstone as the world's first national park indicated that some Americans, including a few political leaders, were listening to what Thoreau, Muir, and these others had to say.

Roosevelt, along with his friend George Bird Grinnell, drew upon these and other writings, as well as their own richly varied experiences with nature, to take the unprecedented step of making protection of nature a social and political cause. Of his time in the Badlands, Roosevelt remarked "the romance of my life began here," and "I never would have been president if it had not been for my experiences in North Dakota." As a hunter, angler, and naturalist, Roosevelt grasped the importance of nature for human life. Though he had studied natural history as an undergraduate at Harvard, believing it would be his life's work, Roosevelt owned a passion for reform and had the will—perhaps a need—to be effective. Rather than pursuing a career as a naturalist, he went into politics. His friend George

Barren-ground caribou

Bird Grinnell, publisher of the widely read magazine *Forest and Stream,* champi-
oned all manner of environmental protection and in 1886 founded the Audubon
Society to combat the slaughter of birds for the millinery trade. Fifteen years later,
TR would find himself with an even greater opportunity. In1901, when he inher-
ited the presidency following the assassination of William McKinley, Roosevelt
declared conservation a matter of federal policy.

Roosevelt backed up his words with an almost dizzying series of conservation
victories. He established in 1903 a federal bird reservation on Pelican Island,
Florida, as a haven for egrets, herons, and other birds sought by plume hunters. In
eight years, Roosevelt authorized 150 million acres in the lower 48 states and
another 85 million in Alaska to be set aside from logging under the Forest Reserve
Act of 1891, compared to a total of 45 million under the three prior presidents. To
these protected lands he added five national parks and 17 national monuments. The
NWR system, though, is arguably TR's greatest legacy. Often using executive order
to circumvent Congress, Roosevelt established 51 wildlife refuges.

The earliest federal wildlife refuges functioned as sanctuaries and little else.
Visitors were rare and recreation was prohibited. Between 1905 and 1912 the first
refuges for big-game species were established—Wichita Mountains in Oklahoma,

the National Bison Range in
Montana, and National Elk
Refuge in Jackson, Wyoming.
In 1924, the first refuge to
include native fish was created;
a corridor some 200 miles
long, the Upper Mississippi
National Wildlife and Fish
Refuge spanned the states of
Minnesota, Wisconsin, Illi-
nois, and Iowa.

Still, the 1920s were dark
years for America's wildlife.
The effects of unregulated
hunting, along with poor
enforcement of existing laws,
had decimated once-abundant
species. Extinction was feared
for the wood duck. Wild turkey

Atlantic puffins, Petit Manan NWR, Maine

had become scarce outside a few southern states. Pronghorn antelope, which today
number perhaps a million across the West, were estimated at 25,000 or fewer. The
trumpeter swan, canvasback duck, even the prolific and adaptable white-tailed
deer, were scarce or extirpated across much of their historic ranges.

The Depression and Dust-bowl years, combined with the leadership of
President Franklin Delano Roosevelt, gave American conservation—and the
refuge system in particular—a hefty forward push. As wetlands vanished and fertile prairie soils blew away, FDR's Civilian Conservation Corps (CCC) dispatched
thousands of unemployed young men to camps that stretched from Georgia to
California. On the sites of many present-day refuges, they built dikes and other

Saguaro cactus and ocotillo along Charlie Bell 4WD trail, Cabeza Prieta NWR, Arizona.

water-control structures, planted shelterbelts and grasses. Comprised largely of men from urban areas, the experience of nature was no doubt a powerful rediscovery of place and history for the CCC generation. The value of public lands as a haven for people, along with wildlife, was on the rise.

In 1934, Jay Norwood "Ding" Darling was instrumental in developing the federal "Duck Stamp," a kind of war bond for wetlands; hunters were required to purchase it, and anyone else who wished to support the cause of habitat acquisition could, too. Coupled with the Resettlement Act of 1935, in which the federal government bought out or condemned private land deemed unsuitable for agriculture, several million acres of homesteaded or settled lands reverted to federal ownership to become parks, national grasslands, and wildlife refuges. The Chief of the U.S. Biological Survey's Wildlife Refuge Program, J. Clark Salyer, set out on a cross-country mission to identify prime wetlands. Salyer's work added 600,000 acres to the refuge system, including Red Rock Lakes in Montana, home to a small surviving flock of trumpeter swans.

The environmental ruin of the Dust bowl also set in motion an era of government initiatives to engineer solutions to such natural events as floods, drought, and the watering of crops. Under FDR, huge regional entities such as the Tennessee Valley Authority grew, and the nation's mightiest rivers—the Columbia, Colorado, and later, the Missouri—were harnessed by dams. In the wake of these and other federal works projects, a new concept called "mitigation" appeared: If a proposed dam or highway caused the destruction of a certain number of acres of wetlands or other habitat, some amount of land nearby would be ceded to conservation in return. A good many of today's refuges were the progeny of mitigation. The federal government, like the society it represents, was on its way to becoming complex enough that the objectives of one arm could be at odds with those of another.

Citizen activism, so integral to the rise of the Audubon Society and other groups, was a driving force in the refuge system as well. Residents of rural Georgia applied relentless pressure on legislators to protect the Okefenokee Swamp. Many other refuges—San Francisco Bay, Sanibel Island, Minnesota Valley, New Jersey's Great Swamp—came about through the efforts of people with a vision of conservation close to home.

More than any other federal conservation program, refuge lands became places where a wide variety of management techniques could be tested and refined. Generally, the National Park system followed the "hands off" approach of Muir and Thoreau while the U.S. Forest Service and Bureau of Land Management, in theory, emphasized a utilitarian, "sustainable yield" value; in practice, powerful economic interests backed by often ruthless politics left watersheds, forests, and grasslands badly degraded, with far-reaching consequences for fish and wildlife. The refuge system was not immune to private enterprise—between 1939 and 1945, refuge lands were declared fair game for oil drilling, natural-gas exploration, and even for bombing practice by the U.S. Air Force—but the negative impacts have seldom reached the levels of other federal areas.

Visitor use at refuges tripled in the 1950s, rose steadily through the 1960s, and by the 1970s nearly tripled again. The 1962 Refuge Recreation Act established guidelines for recreational use where activities such as hiking, photography, boating, and camping did not interfere with conservation. With visitors came opportunities to educate, and now nature trails and auto tours, in addition to beauty, offered messages about habitats and management techniques. Public awareness of wilderness, "a place where man is only a visitor," in the words of long-time advocate Robert Marshall of the U.S. Forest Service, gained increasing social and political attention. In 1964, Congress passed the Wilderness Act, establishing guidelines for designating a host of federally owned lands as off-limits to motorized vehicles, road building, and resource exploitation. A large number of refuge lands qualified—the sun-blasted desert of Arizona's Havasu refuge, the glorious tannin-stained waters and cypress forests of Georgia's Okefenokee Swamp, and the almost incomprehensible large 8-million-acre Arctic NWR in Alaska, home to vast herds of caribou, wolf packs, and bladelike mountain peaks, the largest contiguous piece of wilderness in the refuge system.

Sachuest Point NWR, Rhode Island

Nonetheless, this was also a time of horrendous air and water degradation, with the nation at its industrial zenith and agriculture cranked up to the level of "agribusiness." A wake-up call arrived in the form of vanishing bald eagles, peregrine falcons, and osprey. The insecticide DDT, developed in 1939 and used in World War II to eradicate disease-spreading insects, had been used throughout the nation ever since, with consequences unforeseen until the 1960s. Sprayed over wetlands, streams, and crop fields, DDT had entered watersheds and from there the food chain itself. It accumulated in the bodies of fish and other aquatic life, and birds consuming fish took DDT into their systems, one effect was a calcium deficiency, resulting in eggs so fragile that female birds crushed them during incubation.

Partially submerged alligator, Anahuac NWR, Texas

Powerful government and industry leaders launched a vicious, all-out attack on the work of a marine scientist named Rachel Carson, whose book *Silent Spring*, published in 1962, warned of the global dangers associated with DDT and other biocides. For this she was labeled "not a real scientist" and "a hysterical woman." With eloquence and courage, though, Carson stood her ground. If wild species atop the food chain could be devastated, human life could be threatened, too. Americans were stunned, and demanded an immediate ban on DDT. Almost overnight, the "web of life" went from chalkboard hypothesis to reality.

Protecting imperiled species became a matter of national policy in 1973 when President Nixon signed into law the Endangered Species Act (ESA), setting guidelines by which the U.S. Fish & Wildlife Service would "list" plant and animal species as *threatened* or *endangered* and would develop a program for their recovery. Some 56 refuges, such as Ash Meadows in Nevada and Florida's Crystal River, home of the manatee, were established specifically for the protection of endangered species. Iowa's tiny Driftless Prairie refuge exists to protect the rare, beautifully colored pleistocene land snail and a wildflower, the northern monkshood. Sometimes unwieldy, forever politicized, the ESA stands as a monumental achievement. Its successes include the American alligator, bald eagle, and gray wolf. The whooping crane would almost surely be extinct today without the twin supports of ESA and the refuge system. The black-footed ferret, among the rarest mammals on earth, is today being reintroduced on a few western refuges. In 1998, nearly one-fourth of all threatened and endangered species populations find sanctuary on refuge lands.

The 1980s and '90s have brought no end of conservation challenges, faced by an increasingly diverse association of organizations and strategies. Partnerships now link the refuge system with nonprofit groups, from Ducks Unlimited and The Nature Conservancy to international efforts such as Partners in Flight, a program to monitor the decline of, and to secure habitat for, neotropical songbirds. These cooperative efforts have resulted in habitat acquisition and restoration, research, and many new refuges. Partnerships with private landowners who voluntarily offer marginally useful lands for restoration—with a sponsoring conservation group cost-sharing the project—have revived many thousands of acres of grasslands, wetlands, and riparian corridors.

Coyote on the winter range

Citizen activism is alive and well as we enter the new millennium. Protecting and promoting the growth of the NWR system is a primary campaign of the National Audubon Society, which, by the year 2000, will have grown to a membership of around 550,000. NAS itself also manages about 100 sanctuaries and nature centers across the country, with a range of opportunities for environmental education. The National Wildlife Refuge Association, a volunteer network, keeps members informed of refuge events, environmental issues, and legislative developments and helps to maintain a refuge volunteer workforce. In 1998, a remarkable 20 percent of all labor performed on the nation's refuges was carried out by volunteers, a contribution worth an estimated $14 million.

A national wildlife refuge today has many facets. Nature is ascendant and thriving, often to a shocking degree when compared with adjacent lands. Each site has its own story: a prehistory, a recent past, a present—a story of place, involving people, nature, and stewardship, sometimes displayed in Visitor Center or Headquarters exhibits, always written into the landscape. Invariably a refuge belongs to a community as well, involving area residents who visit, volunteers who log hundreds of hours, and a refuge staff who are knowledgeable and typically friendly, even outgoing, especially if the refuge is far-flung. In this respect most every refuge is a portal to local culture, be it Native American, cows and crops, or big city. There may be no better example of democracy in action than a national wildlife refuge. The worm-dunker fishes while a mountain biker pedals past. In spring, birders scan marshes and grasslands that in the fall will be walked by hunters. Compromise is the guiding principle.

What is the future of the NWR system? In Prairie City, Iowa, the Neal Smith

NWR represents a significant departure from the time-honored model. Established in 1991, the site had almost nothing to "preserve." It was old farmland with scattered remnants of tallgrass prairie and degraded oak savanna. What is happening at Neal Smith, in ecological terms, has never been attempted on such a scale: the reconstruction, essentially from scratch, of a self-sustaining 8,000-acre native biome, complete with bison and elk, greater prairie chickens, and a palette of wildflowers and grasses that astonish and delight.

What is happening in human terms is equally profound. Teams of area residents, called "seed seekers," explore cemeteries, roadside ditches, and long-ignored patches of ground. Here and there they find seeds of memory, grasses and wildflowers from the ancient prairie, and harvest them; the seeds are catalogued and planted on the refuge. The expanding prairie at Neal Smith is at once new and very old. It is reshaping thousands of Iowans' sense of place, connecting them to what was, eliciting wonder for what could be. And the lessons here transcend biology. In discovering rare plants, species found only in the immediate area, people discover an identity beyond job titles and net worth. The often grueling labor of cutting brush, pulling nonnative plants, and tilling ground evokes the determined optimism of Theodore and Franklin Roosevelt and of the CCC.

As the nation runs out of wild places worthy of preservation, might large-scale restoration of damaged or abandoned lands become the next era of American conservation? There are ample social and economic justifications. The ecological justifications are endless, for, as the history of conservation and ecology has revealed, nature and humanity cannot go their separate ways. The possibilities, if not endless, remain rich for the years ahead.

—*John Grassy*

How to use this book

Local conditions and regulations on national wildlife refuges vary considerably. We provide detailed, site-specific information useful for a good refuge visit, and we note the broad consistencies throughout the NWR system (facility set-up and management, what visitors may or may not do, etc.). Contact the refuge before arriving or stop by the Visitor Center when you get there. F&W wildlife refuge managers are ready to provide friendly, savvy advice about species and habitats, plus auto, hiking, biking, or water routes that are open and passable, and public programs (such as guided walks) you may want to join.

AUDUBON GUIDES TO THE NATIONAL WILDLIFE REFUGES

This is one of nine regional volumes in a series covering the entire NWR system. **Visitable refuges**—over 300 of them—constitute about three-fifths of the NWR system. **Nonvisitable refuges** may be small (without visitor facilities), fragile (set up to protect an endangered species or threatened habitat), or new and undeveloped.

Among visitable refuges, some are more important and better developed than others. In creating this series, we have categorized refuges as A, B, or C level, with the A-level refuges getting the most attention. You will easily recognize the difference. C-level refuges, for instance, do not carry a map.

Rankings can be debated; we know that. We considered visitation statistics, accessibility, programming, facilities, and the richness of the refuges' habitats and animal life. Some refuges ranked as C-level now may develop further over time.

Many bigger NWRs have either "satellites" (with their own refuge names) separate "units" within the primary refuge or other, less significant NWRs nearby. All of these, at times, were deemed worthy of a brief mention.

THE ORGANIZATION OF THE BOOK

■ **REGIONAL OVERVIEW** This regional introduction is intended to give readers the big picture, touching on broad patterns in landscape formation, interconnections among plant communities, and diversity of animals. We situate NWRs in the natural world of the larger bio-region to which they belong, showing why these federally protected properties stand out as wild places worth preserving amid encroaching civilization.

We also note some wildlife management issues that will surely color the debate around campfires and congressional conference tables in years ahead, while paying recognition to the NWR supporters and managers who helped make the present refuge system a reality.

ABOUT THE U.S. FISH & WILDLIFE SERVICE Under the Department of the Interior, the U.S. Fish & Wildlife Service is the principal federal agency responsible for conserving and protecting wildlife and plants and their habitats for the benefit of the American people. The Service manages the 93-million-acre NWR system, comprised of more than 500 national wildlife refuges, thousands of small wetlands, and other special management areas. It also operates 66 national fish hatcheries, 64 U.S. Fish & Wildlife Management Assistance offices, and 78 ecological services field stations. The agency enforces federal wildlife laws, administers the Endangered Species Act, manages migratory bird populations, restores nationally significant fisheries, conserves and restores wildlife habitats such as wetlands, and helps foreign governments with their conservation efforts. It also oversees the federal-aid program that distributes hundreds of millions of dollars in excise taxes on fishing and hunting equipment to state wildlife agencies.

■ **THE REFUGES** The refuge section of the book is organized alphabetically by state and then, within each state, by refuge name.

There are some clusters, groups, or complexes of neighboring refuges administered by one primary refuge. Some refuge complexes are alphabetized here by the name of their primary refuge, with the other refuges in the group following immediately thereafter.

■ **APPENDIX**

Nonvisitable National Wildlife Refuges: NWR properties that meet the needs of wildlife but are off-limits to all but field biologists.

Federal Recreation Fees: An overview of fees and fee passes.

Volunteer Activities: How you can lend a hand to help your local refuge or get involved in supporting the entire NWR system.

U.S. Fish & Wildlife General Infromation: The seven regional head-quarters of the U.S. Fish & Wildlife Service through which the National Wildlife Refuge System is administered.

National Audubon Society Wildlife Sanctuaries: A listing of the 24 National Audubon Society wildlife sanctuaries, dispersed across the U.S., which are open to the public.

Bibliography & Resources: Natural-history titles both on the region generally and its NWRs, along with a few books of inspiration about exploring the natural world.

Glossary: A listing of specialized terms (not defined in the text) tailored to this region.

Index

National Audubon Society Mission Statement

PRESENTATION OF INFORMATION: A-LEVEL REFUGE

■ **INTRODUCTION** This section attempts to evoke the essence of the place, The writer sketches the sounds or sights you might experience on the refuge, such as sandhill cranes taking off, en masse, from the marsh, filling the air with the roar of thousands of beating wings. That's a defining event for a particular refuge and a great reason to go out and see it.

■ **MAP** Some refuges are just a few acres; several, like the Alaskan behemoths, are bigger than several eastern states. The scale of the maps in this series can vary. We recommend that you also ask refuges for their detailed local maps.

■ **HISTORY** This outlines how the property came into the NWR system and what its uses were in the past.

■ **GETTING THERE** General location; seasons and hours of operation; fees, if any (see federal recreation fees in Appendix); address, telephone. Smaller or remote refuges may have their headquarters off-site. We identify highways as follows: TX14 = Texas state highway # 14; US 23 = a federal highway; I-85 = Interstate 85.

Note: Many NWRs have their own web pages at the F&W web site, http://www.fws.gov/. Some can be contacted by fax or e-mail, and if we do not provide that information here, you may find it at the F&W web site.

■ **TOURING** The **Visitor Center**, if there is one, is the place to start your tour. Some have wildlife exhibits, videos, and bookstores; others may be only a kiosk. Let someone know your itinerary before heading out on a long trail or into the backcountry, and then go explore.

Most refuges have roads open to the public; many offer a wildlife **auto tour,** with wildlife information signs posted en route or a brochure or audiocassette to guide you. Your car serves as a bird blind if you park and remain quiet. Some refuge roads require 4-wheel-drive or a high-chassis vehicle. Some roads are closed seasonally to protect habitats during nesting seasons or after heavy rain or snow.

Touring also covers **walking and hiking** (see more trail details under ACTIV-ITIES) and **biking.** Many refuge roads are rough; mountain or hybrid bikes are more appropriate than road bikes. When water is navigable, we note what kinds of **boats** may be used and where there are boat launches.

■ **WHAT TO SEE**

Landscape and climate: This section covers geology, topography, and climate: primal forces and raw materials that shaped the habitats that lured species to the refuge. It also includes weather information for visitors.

Plant life: This is a sampling of noteworthy plants on the refuge, usually sorted by habitat, using standard botanical nomenclature. Green plants bordering watery places are in "Riparian Zones"; dwarfed trees, shrubs, and flowers on windswept mountaintops are in the "Alpine Forest"; and so forth.

Wildflowers abound, and you may want to see them in bloom. We give advice about timing your visit, but ask the refuge for more. If botany and habitat relationships are new to you, you can soon learn to read the landscape as a set of interrelated communities. Take a guided nature walk to begin.

(Note: In two volumes, "Plants" is called "Habitats and Plant Communities.")

Animal life: The national map on pages 4 and 5 shows the major North American "flyways." Many NWRs cluster in watery territory underneath the birds' aerial superhighways. There are many birds in this book, worth seeing simply for their beauty. But ponder, too, what birds eat (fish, insects, aquatic plants), or how one species (the mouse) attracts another (the fox), and so on up the food chain, and you'll soon understand the rich interdependence on display in many refuges.

Animals use camouflage and stealth for protection; many are nocturnal. You may want to come out early or late to increase your chances of spotting them. Refuge managers can offer advice on sighting or tracking animals.

Grizzly bears, venomous snakes, alligators, and crocodiles can indeed be dangerous. Newcomers to these animals' habitats should speak with refuge staff about precautions before proceeding.

■ **ACTIVITIES** Some refuges function not only as wildlife preserves but also as recreation parks. Visit a beach, take a bike ride, and camp overnight, or devote your time to serious wildlife observation.

Camping and swimming: If not permissible on the refuge, there may be federal or state campgrounds nearby; we mention some of them. Planning an NWR camping trip should start with a call to refuge headquarters.

Wildlife observation: This subsection touches on strategies for finding species most people want to see. Crowds do not mix well with certain species; you

---

A NOTE ON HUNTING AND FISHING Opinions on hunting and fishing on federally owned wildlife preserves range from "Let's have none of it" to "We need it as part of the refuge management plan." The F&W Service follows the latter approach, with about 290 hunting programs and 260 fishing programs. If you have strong opinions on this topic, talk with refuge managers to gain some insight into F&W's rationale. You can also write to your representative or your senators in Washington.

For most refuges, we summarize the highlights of the hunting and fishing options. You must first have required state and local licenses for hunting or fishing. Then you must check with refuge headquarters about special restrictions that may apply on the refuge; refuge bag limits, for example, or duration of season may be different from regulations elsewhere in the same state.

Hunting and fishing options change from year to year on many refuges, based on the size of the herd or of the flock of migrating birds. These changes may reflect local weather (a hard winter trims the herd) or disease, or factors in distant habitats where animals summer or winter. We suggest what the options usually are on a given refuge (e.g., some birds, some mammals, fish, but not all etc..). It's the responsibility of those who wish to hunt and fish to confirm current information with refuge headquarters and to abide by current rules.

COMMON SENSE, WORTH REPEATING

Leave no trace Every visitor deserves a chance to see the refuge in its pristine state. We all share the responsibility to minimize our impact on the landscape. "Take only pictures and leave only footprints," and even there you'll want to avoid trampling plant life by staying on established trails. Pack out whatever you pack in. Ask refuge managers for guidance on low-impact hiking and camping.

Respect private property Many refuges consist of noncontiguous parcels of land, with private properties abutting refuge lands. Respect all Private Property and No Trespassing signs, especially in areas where native peoples live within refuge territory and hunt or fish on their own land.

Water Protect the water supply. Don't wash dishes or dispose of human waste within 200 ft. of any water. Treat all water for drinking with iodine tablets, backpacker's water filter, or boiling. Clear water you think is OK may be contaminated upstream by wildlife you cannot see.

may need to go away from established observation platforms to have success. Learn a bit about an animal's habits, where it hunts or sleeps, what time of day it moves about. Adjust your expectations to match the creature's behavior, and your chances of success will improve.

Photography: This section outlines good places or times to see certain species. If you have a zoom lens, use it. Sit still, be quiet, and hide yourself. Don't approach the wildlife; let it approach you. Never feed animals or pick growing plants.

Hikes and walks: Here we list specific outings, with mileages and trailhead locations. Smooth trails and boardwalks, suitable for people with disabilities, are noted. On bigger refuges, there may be many trails. Ask for a local map. If you go bushwacking, first make sure this is permissible. Always carry a map and compass.

Seasonal events: National Wildlife Refuge Week, in October, is widely celebrated, with guided walks, lectures, demonstrations, and activities of special interest to children. Call your local refuge for particulars. At other times of the year there are fishing derbies, festivals celebrating the return of migrating birds, and other events linked to the natural world. Increasingly, refuges post event schedules on their web pages.

Publications: Many NWR brochures are free, such as bird and wildflower checklists. Some refuges have pamphlets and books for sale, describing local habitats and species.

Note: The categories of information above appear in A and B refuges in this book; on C-level refuges, options are fewer, and some of these headings may not appear.

—David Emblidge

New England
A Regional Overview

For many, New England is epitomized by the grand spectacle of its fall foliage. In September and October, vast birch, beech, and maple woodlands are ablaze in hues of gold, orange, bronze, crimson, and purple. The woodlands form the back-drop for other quintessential New England icons: twisting country roads, cozy green hamlets, neat Colonial homes, and the ubiquitous white church spire rising teasingly above the treeline. These regional symbols have found their way into the national psyche for decades—and for good reason: They are an enchanting and elemental part of the landscape.

But Connecticut, Maine, Massachusetts, New Hampshire, Rhode Island, and Vermont—which all together, at 350 by 450 miles, could fit within the state of Missouri—also offer a remarkable biodiversity, supported by coastal plains, ver-dant hills, and mountain valleys. From the pygmy shrew, weighing less than one-tenth of an ounce, to the 50-ton fin whale; from the wind-combed dunes on Cape Cod and its islands to the granite outcrops on the Presidential Range in the White Mountains; from the lush salt marshes limning the Atlantic to the dark evergreen forest along Maine's northern coast, New England is not only one of the most beautiful areas of the country but also one of its most varied bioregions.

Some of the very best places to sample this diversity up close are the 18 National Wildlife Refuges located here—at 60,000 acres, a modest but important piece of the national system's 92 million acres. Habitats change dramatically as New Eng-land refuges climb from warmer coastal properties at sea level to the windswept summit of Wapack NWR's North Pack Monadnock in southwestern New Hamp-shire—at 2,278 feet, the only mountain within a New England refuge. Annually, more than 1 million visitors head outside to the refuges in New England to amble along the beaches, watch a fascinating diversity of wildlife, hike woodland and mountain trails, and boat and fish along sections of the region's 5,400 miles of highly corrugated coastline, or in parts of innumerable rivers, lakes, and ponds.

Indeed, two-thirds of New England's refuges are coastal, an indication of how integral the shoreline marine communities have been to a region that was among the first in the New World to be settled by 17th-century Europeans. Above this coastal terrain is the Atlantic flyway, a superhighway in the sky for migratory waterfowl. Some refuges protect fragile barrier beaches and others include salt marshes, one of the most biologically productive ecosystems on the planet. Still others boast estuaries where rivers flow into the sea, intermingling fresh water with salt, spawning a whole new realm of ecological niches. North of Cape Cod, the shoreline becomes ever bonier as gran-

Winter at Missisquoi NWR, Vermont   ite promontories replace surf-washed beaches. The landscape undergoes another transformation on the Vermont-Quebec border, where a vast freshwater marsh awaits visitors at the Missisquoi refuge. Throughout, the refuge system threads its way, providing essential migration corridors that help ensure species survival.

The newest of the region's refuges is the as yet tiny Silvio O. Conte National Fish & Wildlife Refuge, which refuge managers hope to extend along the Connecticut River, smack amid heavily populated and industrialized communities. New England's largest (24,446 acres), most remote refuge is northeastern Maine's Moosehorn National Wildlife Refuge, as far "down east" as you can go before bumping into New Brunswick.

For the outdoor enthusiast with diverse interests in contrasting landscapes and habitats, natural communities, short walks, and weeklong camping trips, New England's small but choice number of national wildlife refuges serve up an unsuspected cornucopia, all within a day's drive of some of the largest urban centers in the country. On a one-day visit to a coastal New England refuge such as Monomoy, in Massachusetts, sights both minuscule (the tiny white mudwort plant, clinging to grassy mats on the sand) and panoramic (vast flocks of migrant plovers and sandpipers wheeling across the sky) will intrigue and delight all who make the trip. And that is just the beginning.

GEOLOGY

New England was born of fire and ice. The gargantuan collision of North America and Africa 225 million years ago buckled the continent, creating the Appalachian mountain chain. (Continents, after all, are merely riding on the backs of Earth's tectonic plates, plates that are forever sliding under and over each other along their edges at about the same speed that our toenails grow: three-quarters of an inch per year. That friction produces incredible heat, molten rock, volcanoes, and earthquakes.) Erosion began to wear away at the jagged peaks rising up 20,000 feet. Over countless millenia, wind and water wore them down, conveying the grit to the sea.

Then, 500,000 years ago, the first of four mile-thick ice sheets ground its way inexorably southward as Earth's climate cooled. In the four times the ice rode over all of what is now New England, it plucked boulders from the summits and broadened river valleys. When a warming climate ended their reign, at least for the time being (only 10,000 years ago), meltwaters formed vast lakes and the mounds of water-sorted debris (moraines, eskers, kames, and drumlins) were left on the altered landscape that we see today.

But it is not the collision of tectonic plates that effects the most active physical change on the New England coastline; it is the constant flux of water and wind. Unlike mountain-building cataclysms or scouring glacial ice, the relentless action of ocean currents deposits sand to form barrier islands within the blink of an eye—a human lifetime. And even more quickly than they form, powerful storms knock them down like sand castles so that the never-ending process may begin anew.

CLIMATE AND WEATHER

Some of the planet's fiercest weather occurs on the upper reaches of New Hampshire's Mt. Washington (6,290 feet). Here the highest nontornadic winds ever recorded on earth—231 miles per hour—were clocked in 1934. Indeed, the climate of Mount Washington is more polar than temperate. The rest of New England is more benign, although northern New England winters are typically long, cold, and snowy; in early 1999, one northern Maine outpost recorded a bone-chilling 55 degrees F below zero; but this is the rare extreme.

As a rule of thumb, you will experience a one-degree temperature drop for every 400 feet that you ascend in New England, the equivalent of traveling 100 miles north. And depending on exposure—whether a slope is north- or south-facing, for instance—the microclimate can vary considerably, even within a small geographic area. Even so, the region's average winter temperature is below freezing. Quintessential New England winter storms, dubbed nor'easters because of the direction from which their winds blow, form off the coast and sometimes cause considerable coastal flooding or heavy snow. Although a hurricane is generally a tropical weather phenomenon, a powerful storm does strike this coast on occasion. The infamous hurricane of 1938, which destroyed property, devastated forests, and took a heavy toll of human life, remains the worst within memory.

The region's prevailing weather fronts arrive from the west, but the climate,

Moose roam the northern forests of Maine, New Hampshire, and Vermont.

18

NEW ENGLAND

Burlington

Montpelier ★

Vermont

Rutland

17

Augusta ★

Lewiston ●

Portland ●

2

New Hampshire

Concord ★

Manchester ●

12

Nashua ●

11

6

10

Massachusetts

7

Boston ★

Springfield ●

Worcester ●

Hartford ★

Providence ★

Warwick ●

Connecticut

1

New Haven ●

Bridgeport ●

14 16

15

13

8

9

Rhode Island

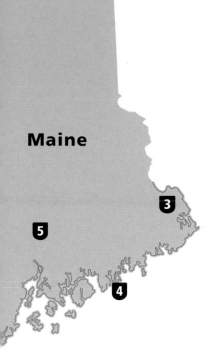

Maine

NEW ENGLAND

CONNECTICUT
1 Stewart B. McKinney NWR

MAINE
2 Rachel Carson NWR
3 Moosehorn NWR
4 Petit Manan NWR
5 Sunkhaze Meadows NWR

MASSACHUSETTS
6 Silvio O. Conte NF & WR
7 Great Meadows NWR
8 Monomoy NWR
9 Nantucket NWR
10 Oxbow NWR
11 Parker River NWR

NEW HAMPSHIRE
12 Wapack NWR

RHODE ISLAND
13 Block Island NWR
14 Ninigret NWR
15 Sachuest NWR
16 Trustom Pond NWR

VERMONT
17 Missisquoi NWR

especially near the coast, is also strongly influenced by two important ocean currents, one cold, the other relatively warm. The Labrador Current shunts cold Arctic waters south and influences the coast as far south as Cape Cod Bay. By contrast, the Gulf Stream is a river of warm subtropical water that moves up the East Coast as far north as southern New England, where land deflects it out into the North Atlantic. Spring along the New England coast tends to be cooler than that of inland areas; fall along the coast is balmy compared with chilly inland autumns. Coastal areas generally receive more precipitation because of the huge quantity of moisture that evaporates from the sea. Cape Cod enjoys the region's mildest climate, a far cry from the brutal winter cold of interior northern Maine.

The climate of New England seems to be moderating, as it is in much of the world. Annual mean temperatures have risen several degrees during just the past century, a trend that, should it continue, will have profound effects on the region's plant and animal life.

HABITATS/BIOMES

■ **FRESHWATER WETLANDS** Bogs are New England's most unusual wetlands. Their formation evolved from the tendency of glacial relics to perch on acidic granite bedrock. Because acids retard decay, organic matter accumulates in bogs. Thick spongy mats of sphagnum moss, capable of holding an amazing 250 times its weight in water, form veritable floating carpets over most bogs. Acid-tolerant plants take root in the mat, coping with the lack of available nitrogen in fascinating ways. Visit Moosehorn NWR to see bog wetlands.

Far more prevalent and familiar are the marshes and swamps once regarded as wasteland fit only for filling. Fortunately, their value in flood control, water purification and recharge, and wildlife habitat creation has since been acknowledged. Whereas cattails, sedges, and other nonwoody plants make a marsh, swamps by definition sport trees and shrubs. Massachusetts's Great Meadows NWR and Vermont's Missisquoi NWR are great places to experience them.

Easily overlooked are the small woodland ponds that usually disappear by late summer. Vernal pools, too, are now receiving long overdue attention; they are the habitat for certain amphibians and other creatures that can perpetuate themselves only there.

■ **GRASSLANDS** Grassland is a rare commodity in heavily wooded New England. Most grasslands are modest in size, especially when compared with vast midcontinent prairies. Primarily coastal, they thrive on sandy soils that have never encouraged tall trees. You will find artificial grasslands at airports, hayfields, and pastures, but fields left fallow fill quickly with sun-loving pioneers. In most of the region annual mowing is required to keep fields from reverting to woodland.

■ **OPEN WATERS** Half the region's refuges hold rivers within their borders, from the 500-mile-long Connecticut River to countless high-gradient, rock-lined, cold-water freshets; others, like southwestern New England's Housatonic River, are languid and meandering. At Maine's Sunkhaze Meadows NWR or Massachusetts' Oxbow NWR, streams are the focal point. Rivers and their watersheds (land areas drained by a river and its tributaries) provide water and habitat for myriad species.

Lakes and ponds figure prominently in New England's landscape and lore, from the vast 400-foot-deep Lake Champlain (only the Great Lakes are larger), in

Boardwalk, Parker River NWR, Massachusetts

northwest Vermont, to Rhode Island's threatened coastal salt ponds, to countless 4-foot-deep beaver ponds. All eventually fill with silt and organic matter brought them by feeder streams. Some of the most fertile croplands initially farmed by European colonists were former beaver ponds.

■ **FORESTS** Boreal forest, New England's true and evocative northwoods, covers only about 20 percent of northern New England. With the exception of Maine's downeast coastline, portions of northwestern Maine, far northern New Hampshire, and extreme northeastern Vermont, this dark, dank, spruce-fir forest is confined to the loftiest summits. Few plants can abide in the year-round shade cast by the evergreens and the acid soil they help form.

The forest with the greatest coverage (and the one pictured on the stereotypical calendar scenes of New England) is northern hardwood, blanketing roughly two-thirds of the entire region, especially in northern and western New England.

This birch-beech-maple woodland is responsible for the region's glorious fall foliage and ample maple-syrup production. These rich, moist woodlands also put on the finest spring wildflower show of any regional forest type.

Oak-hickory woodlands dominate southern New England—most of Connecticut, Rhode Island, and portions of eastern Massachusetts and southeastern New Hampshire. Oak-hickory woodlands are warmer and drier than northern hardwood stands, and their acidic soils are a result of the generous amount of tannic acid in oak leaves. These acidic soils diminish wildflower diversity.

You will find an intermediate type of forest where northern hardwood and oak-hickory forests intermingle. Transition woodlands (sometimes called pine-oak forest) are common in central and western Massachusetts, southeastern New Hampshire, northwest Connecticut, and along much of the Connecticut River Valley in Vermont.

Modest woodland of scrub oak and pitch pine clothes the coastal sand plain of southeastern Massachusetts. These sandy soils have much in common with deserts. Despite the much higher rainfall, plants living here must cope with reduced soil moisture.

■ **MOUNTAINS** New England peaks are, by western standards, rather unimposing. But the summits of New Hampshire's Presidential Range (including Mt.

Coastal scrubland on the dunes, Block Island NWR, Rhode Island

Washington) and Mt. Katahdin in northern Maine are crowned in true alpine vegetation.

The only mountain summit within a New England NWR is modest North Pack Monadnock in southern New Hampshire's Wapack NWR. Many of the region's peaks and ridges reveal naked bedrock, where glaciers scraped off accumulated soil. These so-called balds are open, grassy places where panoramic views abound.

■ **COASTAL** New England's long and filigreed coastline holds immense historical, cultural, and commercial importance, from rockbound downeast Maine to the sandy flexed arm of Cape Cod and the Islands. A wonderful example of the rugged Maine coast is on display at Petit Manan NWR, a granite limb reaching out into the chilly Gulf of Maine. Rocky shore also occurs in southern New England, as Rhode Island's Sachuest NWR can readily attest. But here, wide sandy strands or cobble beaches prevail. The barrier islands of Parker River NWR and Monomoy NWR in Massachusetts hold back the full onslaught of the sea. That the coastline is gradually submerging is evidenced in Connecticut, where stone walls are now washed by tidal currents, and on New Hampshire's shore, where tree stumps are regularly inundated.

Situated along the region's southern and southeastern coastlines and shielded

by barrier spits and islands are the region's endangered salt marshes. These most productive of biological habitats, washed twice daily by life-giving tides, formed in estuaries where river and sea fashioned a nutritious porridge. Before their importance as nurseries for numerous fin and shellfish was understood, many acres were ditched, drained, and filled.

Just inland from much of southern New England's shore are expanses of coastal scrublands dominated by thickets of berry-producing shrubs that provide food and cover for migrant and resident birds.

HUMAN IMPACT ON LANDSCAPE

Portions of New England have been, as regional road signs warn, "thickly settled" for nearly four centuries. In that time human hands have transformed the landscape dramatically. The indigenous peoples that hunted, gathered, fished, and farmed the region regularly burned coastal grasslands to stimulate the growth of grasses and improve them for game production. That impact, given their relatively low population levels (some estimate about 80,000 people regionwide), was negligible, however, compared with the wholesale impacts wrought by later industrialized and mechanized civilizations.

Only 5 percent of New England's old-growth forests remains—and nearly all of those lie in the far north. In the north, large-scale logging took its toll. Most land in the south was long ago cleared for agriculture and charcoal production (to fuel the iron furnaces). Indeed, the region today is remarkably wooded compared with the rocky agricultural landscape of the early part of the 19th century, when more than three-quarters of southern New England was barren of trees. In a nearly complete turnabout, 75 percent is now wooded.

Much of New England's farmland was abandoned when people flocked to greener pastures in the Midwest, giving the region's woodlands some 130 years to reclaim once barren ground. But because mature forests require hundreds of years to form, it will be at least another century or two before the area once again takes on some semblance of precolonial New England. It takes more than big trees to make an old-growth forest. Even so, reforestation has had profound effects on the region's plant life and, by direct extension, its wildlife.

Creatures once eradicated or considered rare have made incredible comebacks. Humans have had a direct hand in retintroducing the beaver, once virtually trapped to extinction for its luxuriant fur, and have been similarly successful in bringing back the wild turkey. Mammals such as black bear and fisher, which had remained in the far reaches of northern New England, are recolonizing their former haunts in the three southernmost states. The return of the great whales to New England waters has been truly remarkable; other whale species, like the endangered northern right whale, have never recovered from the carnage of 19th-century whaling. Far less obvious but more insidious is the pollution of coastal estuaries by effluent, necessitating the closure of shellfish beds.

A discussion of the human impacts on New England's landscape is hardly complete without mention of the negative impacts so many introduced plant and animal species have had and continue to have. One thousand species native to other parts of the globe, especially Eurasia, have colonized the region, sometimes with very negative outcomes. The choking of freshwater wetlands by purple loosestrife and the deleterious effects of the house sparrow on native cavity-nesting birds are but two examples among many. Recent efforts to combat exotic invaders indicate that there is still hope.

PLANTS

A green blanket of trees covers most of New England, obscuring gray ledge outcrops. Elevation, latitude, moisture, soils, and bedrock together determine which forest type thrives on any given site. And each in turn influences what grows in association with the trees, from mosses to wildflowers to shrubs.

The white pine is Maine's state tree—and with good reason. At the end of the 19th century, Maine led the United States in timber production, and white pine was king. Since before the American Revolution, when any pine greater than 20 inches in diameter was marked as a Crown Tree (for use as sailing-vessel masts and spars), the white pine played a pivotal role. Other conifers have been important in the region's industrial development. The tannin-rich inner bark of eastern hemlock, which thrives in moist, shady environments, was an essential ingredient in the leather-tanning process. American beech was the preferred wood for barrel making, while the nutritious nuts fed numerous mammals and birds, including the now-extinct passenger pigeon. The extensive spruce forests of northern New England provide fodder for the modern pulpwood industry. In southern New England, the massive columnar trunks of yellow poplar (tulip tree) rise high above the moist woods. One hundred feet up they unfurl their big, yellow-green blossoms.

Northern forest wetlands, Moosehorn NWR, Maine

New England's northern hardwoods mount two annual extravaganzas, some six months apart. The kaleidoscopic autumnal light show is world renowned, of course, with sugar maple the star. But in April and May, the forest floor comes alive with delicate wildflowers that use a narrow window of time to bloom, be pollinated, and set seed before the thickening canopy above pulls down the curtain. From hepatica to bloodroot to violet to trillium to orchid, spring flowers debut every few days to delight the eye.

There is something evocative and even magical about heaths—acid-tolerant, woody plants that range in height from 3 inches to 15 feet. Almost all are evergreen, with thickened leaves that retard water loss. Laurel and azalea shrubs grace woodlands and wetlands, respectively, with unrivaled floral bouquets in late spring. One, mountain laurel, is the state flower of Connecticut. Another, of tiny stature, is trailing arbutus, or mayflower, the state flower of Massachusetts. Six-foot highbush blueberry and several species of lowbush blueberry produce delectable fruit while tart cranberries grow in natural bogs and manmade ones that are flooded at harvest time.

Insectivorous bog plants have always held a strange fascination. Seemingly born in some mad scientist's laboratory, pitcher plants and sundews entrap insects in ingenious ways and digest them to extract needed nitrogen—a clever way of coping with the nitrogen-poor bog environment. Although bogs are wet by definition, acid makes it difficult for plants to absorb water.

Salt-marsh ecosystems rest squarely on a foundation of cordgrasses; the decaying grasses provide energy for invertebrates and ultimately the fin and shellfish that feed numerous predators. Salt-marsh plants survive in demanding environments and must cope with alternating desiccation and drowning.

Freshwater wetlands wait until summer to put on their finery. In ponds and sluggish streams, arrowhead, pickerelweed, water lilies, bladderwort, aquatic smartweed, and a host of others brighten the waterways. In shallow water, cattails provide food and shelter for many creatures.

ANIMALS

As New England's once-ravaged woodlands have healed since the middle of the 19th century, the region's mammal population has steadily increased. Black bear are now estimated to number more than 25,000, while fisher numbers exceed 10,000. The burgeoning white-tailed deer population threatens habitat destruction in some areas, with a regionwide population estimated at more than half a million. A relative newcomer is the eastern coyote, bigger than its western cousin and infused with wolf genes. But the ecosytem is still unbalanced. The top carnivores, the timber wolf and mountain lion, have not returned, although reports of cougars from southern New England are on the rise. Jet black ravens grace southern New England skies after an absence of a century, but the eastern timber rattlesnake is endangered and the decline of some amphibians has scientists baffled.

Yet each season holds great promise. Skeins of northbound geese herald spring; many Canadas now nest hundreds of miles south of their former Arctic nesting grounds. Meanwhile, a primal rite of spring plays out under the cover of darkness during the season's first warm rains in late March and early April. Spotted, Jefferson, and blue-spotted salamanders shake off their winter stupor and head to woodland pools where they court, mate, and produce the next generation. Wood frogs join the mating frenzy in these ephemeral pools.

In a scene reminiscent of a primordial earth, massing female horseshoe crabs flood the sandy beaches with thousands of pearly eggs during May's full-moon tide; most fuel northbound sandpipers and plovers who time their migrations accordingly. An ancient urge also sends countless small birds winging north from Mexico, the Caribbean, Central and South America. The relative uniformity of tropical forests is left behind in a mad dash for the temperate woodlands of New England, where nesting activities coincide with bumper insect crops.

Fragile barrier beaches host nesting threatened piping plovers and least terns. Offshore, great whales filter the rich planktonic soup welling up from the depths. Whale-watching has struck a responsive chord with the public; people gaze in wonder at the leviathans of the deep. Seabirds also congregate on the rich feeding grounds, and seals are increasing in number; rocky crags and islets serve as refuges for both. In the northwoods, male moose with water dripping off their massive antlers munch succulent water lilies. With surprising regularity these awkward-looking browsers are appearing in inhabited areas of southern New England.

Coastal wildlife refuges provide much-needed habitats for many species of birds to flourish amid the populated stretches of the New England shoreline; here, the greater yellowleg.

Surely beaver have had the greatest impact on the landscape since their reintroduction early in the 20th century. Streams in suitable habitat have virtually all been dammed by resident beavers. Their ponds benefit a whole spectrum of creatures, from red-spotted newts to mink and great blue herons.

Fall migration begins early for shorebirds. By early July, many adults are already headed south along migration corridors. Along the coast, wheeling flocks of sandpipers and plovers probe the mudflats at low tide for hidden invertebrates. Southbound geese and a menagerie of ducks likewise refuel on refuges before resuming their perilous journeys. Hawks also follow the coastline, feasting on the unwary among the flocks. But birds are not the only sojourners. Orange-and-black monarch butterflies make a monumental autumnal journey of 2,000 miles that takes them to the cool Transvolcanic Mountain Range of central Mexico.

In winter, when their food supplies fail, ghostly snowy owls and keen-eyed rough-legged hawks forsake the Arctic for New England in order to feast on meadow voles in fields and salt marshes. Meanwhile, in deep woodlands, stealthy bobcats pursue snowshoe hares adorned in winter white.

Bay scallop shells, Nantucket NWR, Massachusetts

REGIONAL WILDLIFE MANAGEMENT PRIORITIES

On federal wildlife refuges recreational uses are secondary, as they should be. As one New England NWR manager put it so succinctly in a letter announcing the closure of certain areas on the property, "On national wildlife refuges, wildlife comes first." And this is precisely the charge that the refuge system has been given. The sad truth is that as humans have altered the landscape by removing native predators, introducing exotics, and discharging untreated wastes into the environment, remedial actions have become necessary. The question remains, Are they too little, too late?

The national migratory-bird management program is the leading priority at most, if not all, of the region's refuges. To maintain habitat for migratory waterfowl, resting and feeding habitat for migrant shorebirds, songbirds, and other species is the prime goal. This can take many forms, including combating exotics, invasive species; water-level management; beach closure; monitoring; and, in some instances where endangered or threatened species are vulnerable, control of predators and other species. An example of the latter is the controversial gull-control program carried out at Monomoy NWR in Massachusetts during the late

1990s. Great black-backed and herring gulls, whose numbers had increased expo-nentially in southern New England due largely to the easy pickings afforded at landfills, were significant predators of threatened piping plover and least tern chicks. Control efforts have largely been successful to date.

Managing those same plover and tern beaches for the birds' benefit also puts refuge managers squarely at odds with the recreational pursuits of thousands of people during the spring and summer months as popular beaches are closed for up to five months each year. Beyond closure, nesting areas have also been fenced and posted and shelters for birds have been provided in a largely successful attempt to change the odds in the birds' favor.

Many coastal sites have had to contend with pollution from such "non-point" sources as sewage and stormwater runoff. By contaminating shellfish beds, forcing the closure of clamflats and swimming beaches, impacts have been felt economi-cally as well as biologically. A more obvious form of pollution takes the form of oil spills like the one that fouled the beaches and saltwater ponds of the Rhode Island coast (including those at Trustom Pond NWR) in early 1996. Legislation mandat-ing that oil tankers and barges be double-hulled will eventually lessen this threat.

The recognition that exotic invasive plants and animals are having major dele-terious effects upon our native species has created a growing awareness among managers of conservation lands in New England and elsewhere. Marshes taken over by purple loosestrife; waterways choked with Eurasian millfoil; and wood-lands invaded by Japanese barberry, oriental bittersweet, and a host of other woody invaders indicate that the problem is substantial. The overall result is a loss of native species—a negative impact on biodiversity. At times, herbicides are required to combat the insidious threats posed by exotics that have no predators or diseases on this continent. One need only scan acres and acres of magenta-colored wetlands in summer to grasp the seriousness of the situation. Still, ongo-ing efforts at many properties, such as control of water chestnut at Great Meadows NWR, Massachusetts, are beginning to turn the tide.

This is all part of the habitat restoration efforts at many of New England's wildlife refuges. On some, particular stages of ecological succession are encour-aged in order to benefit a given species or group of species that have been sin-gled out for enhancement. Keeping fields open for courting American woodcock by mowing and burning at Moosehorn NWR in Maine is but one example. Repair of previously diked salt marshes is another. Ditches were once dug in salt marshes in a misguided attempt to remove standing water that harbored salt-marsh mosquito larvae; unfortunately, the ditching also eliminated the habitat of small fish that eat mosquito larvae. In instances where white-tailed deer are alter-ing the landscape for the worse because of selective browsing, control efforts are under way. Efforts to undo these past errors are under way on some properties.

The region's national wildlife refuges are an invaluable resource not just for the countless plants and animals that find refuge there, but also for the many peo-ple who seek recreation, solitude, and perhaps even a rekindling of a primal con-nection with nature.

Stewart B. McKinney NWR
Milford Point Unit, Milford, Connecticut
Salt Meadow Unit, Westbrook, Connecticut

Rugosa Rose Estuary, Milford Point Unit, Stewart B. McKinney NWR

MILFORD POINT UNIT

Developers had long set their sights on the Milford Point peninsula, a natural oasis situated on an intensely populated shoreline. Today, the barrier beach is protected from development and also helps to shield the 865-acre Charles E. Wheeler State Management Area from the storms and tides of Long Island Sound. Even though much of Milford Point is dredge fill, it teems with wildlife and is one of southern New England's finest birding areas.

HISTORY

Congress designated a five-unit complex as Connecticut Coastal NWR in 1984. In 1987, it was renamed in honor of the late U.S. congressman Stewart B. McKinney, who was instrumental in establishing the 22-acre refuge, now one of eight units. A hotel built on the site in 1868 served as a Coast Guard reconnaissance center during World War II. The unit is administered by Ninigret NWR and managed by the Connecticut Audubon Coastal Center (CACC) at Milford Point, just northeast of the Milford Point unit.

GETTING THERE

From I-95, take Exit 34 south to Rte. 1. Go right (southwest) .5 mi. to Naugatuck Ave. Turn left and travel .8 mi. to Milford Point Rd. Turn right on Milford Point Rd. for .5 mi. to Sea View Ave. Turn right and drive .35 mi. to a fork in the road. Take the right fork (left is a private road) to the CACC and the Hubbell Wildlife Sanctuary.

■ **SEASON:** Open Sept.-March Closed April-Aug. (piping plover nesting season; contact refuge manager for dates). CACC and grounds open year-round.

■ **HOURS:** Refuge: 30 minutes before sunrise to 30 minutes after sunset. CACC: Tues.–Sat. 10 a.m.–4 p.m., Sun. noon–4 p.m.; grounds open dawn to dusk.

■ **FEES:** Free access. CACC: entrance fee charged.

■ **ADDRESS:** Stewart B. McKinney NWR, P.O. Box 1030, Westbrook, CT 06498; CACC, 1 Milford Point Rd., Milford, CT 06460.

■ **TELEPHONE, FAX, AND E-MAIL:** Stewart B. McKinney NWR: 860/399-2513; CACC: 860/878-7440; fax: 860/399-2515; e-mail: R5RW_SBMNWR@fws.gov

WHAT TO SEE

■ **LANDSCAPE AND CLIMATE** Milford Point is a narrow hook of sandy barrier beach and low dunes, salt marshes, mudflats, and dredge fill at the mouth of the Housatonic River. It is a landscape made all the more appealing by the elemental fragrances of salt-marsh decay and sea spray.

A .4-mile trail, partly along the shore, leads to the tip of Milford Point. Walk past the Visitor Center, with its 70-foot roofed observation tower, on a path that crosses Smith Point Road and leads to the wide boardwalk that overlooks the beach and the sound. Turn right from the boardwalk and walk below the high-tide line (demarcated by the wrack line) to where the fence meets the water. Turn right and walk away from the beach to a small platform astride the fence that designates the refuge boundary. Picnicking and sunbathing are not permitted.

■ **PLANT LIFE** The long yellow flower-spikes of saltwater cordgrass, the foundation of this ecosystem's food web, populate the productive Nell's Island salt marsh in the Wheeler Management Area. In contrast, dense stands of common reed (up to 12 feet high) indicate saturated, disturbed soils and excess nutrients (sometimes from effluent).

HUNTING AND FISHING Surf fishing is allowed year-round from refuge shores, as are **clamming** and **crabbing** for **blue crabs**. Clamming is regulated by the town of Milford; however, contact the refuge office for instructions on applying for a permit. **Fishing** by boat on the Menunketesuck River is popular, and anglers most frequently hook **striped bass, bluefish**, and **flounder**. Please note that the shores are prone to frequent closures to fishing due to high levels of water pollution. Contact the refuge for the latest closures. **Hunting** is not allowed at the McKinney refuge.

American beach grass, which requires constant burial by sand to survive and prosper, binds the point together. Showy seaside goldenrod, yellow evening primrose, and pink beach pea bloom beyond the beach.

The disturbed soils of the peninsula, consisting largely of fill from elsewhere, provide suitable growing conditions for many alien species. Migrating monarch butterflies favor the pink thistlelike flowers of the spotted knapweed. The loveliest exotics are the large bushes of saltspray (rugosa) rose; the 3-inch-diameter fragrant pink blossoms produce plump red hips. Clumps of fast-growing, pollution-resistant ailanthus trees, natives of China, thrive also.

■ **ANIMAL LIFE**

Birds Late summer and early fall are wonderful seasons for birdwatching on the Housatonic delta. Watch for ospreys plunging feet first into the water to gaff fish. Big black double-crested cormorants (crests visible during breeding season only) sometimes swim with only their heads and long necks visible; they propel their sleek bodies with powerful kicks. Egrets and herons feed on fish, frogs, crabs, and other delicacies. Piping plovers and least terns breed on the beaches from April to August. Myriad shorebirds feed and rest in late summer.

Black ducks breed in this estuary, as do huge white mute swans, beautiful but destructive nonnatives. The giant birds have wingspans of 6¾ to 7¾ feet. They consume a great amount of vegetative material, which is transformed into a great quantity of waste. The waste is full of nutrients that can cause algal blooms in the ponds and rob them of oxygen, which is deleterious to aquatic creatures. They have no natural enemies and, by their size and aggressiveness, may displace native waterfowl.

Marine life and mammals At low tide, the entrances to the round burrows of the tiny sand fiddler crabs are littered with half-inch balls of processed sand from which the crabs have removed algae and other microscopic tidbits. The crabs, named for the one huge claw with which males fight for dominion, are very alert. They will dash for cover as you approach. Remain still for five minutes, and they cautiously emerge.

A search of the tidal flats will turn up long thin shells of razor clams, round moon snails, blood arks, false angel wings, and claws of black-fingered mud crabs, lady crabs, and green crabs. At the upper reaches of the flats, the leafless and succulent glasswort (pickleweed) pokes up from the mud; salty fluid fills its edible translucent stems. In late summer glasswort turns red.

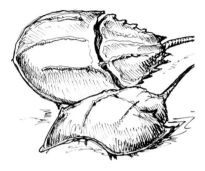

At low tide mud dog-whelks (not true whelks) swarm onto the mudflats to graze on algae. These small scav-

Horseshoe crabs

enging snails become escargot themselves for black ducks, egrets, and muskrats.

Walk along the beach to find oysters, ribbed and blue mussels, slipper (or boat) shells, jingle shells, and quahogs, as well as blue crabs and horseshoe crabs (not really a crab at all). Turn over a board and discover runways lined with grass clippings and other signs of meadow voles.

SALT MEADOW UNIT

Gently rolling uplands hold towering hardwood trees and stone walls that once bounded pastures. Below the canopy a sun-flecked forest floor gives life to a thriving community of plants and animals. This land shows the telltale effects of glacial ice: errant boulders scattered through the woodland. And bordering terra firma, a rehabilitated salt marsh, inundated and exposed twice daily by the tides, provides sustenance for creatures as diverse as mummichogs (small fish living in the salt marsh) and dazzling snowy egrets.

HISTORY

The property was donated in 1971 by Esther Lape, a friend of Mrs. Eleanor Roosevelt's and an adviser on public-health issues to President Franklin

Roosevelt. Mrs. Roosevelt visited here often. A lovely historic brick manor house on Murdock Hill, replete with wrought-iron balcony, was constructed in 1929 and serves as the headquarters and Visitor Center. An adjacent log cabin also remains. Vestiges of formal gardens and a fountain are visible from the trails of this 247-acre refuge.

Once a unit of Ninigret NWR, Salt Meadow is now part of the Stewart B. McKinney NWR along with Milford Point and six other coastal units. About 12,000 people visit these units each year.

Visitor Center, Salt Meadow Unit, Stewart B. McKinney NWR

GETTING THERE

From Exit 64 of I-95 (Connecticut Turnpike), turn south and proceed less than 0.1 mi. to a four-way flashing red light. Turn left (east) onto Old Clinton Rd. and travel 1.1 mi. to the refuge parking area on the right.

■ **SEASON:** Refuge open year-round.

■ **HOURS:** Refuge open one-half hour before sunrise to one-half hour after sunset. Visitor Center open weekdays 8 a.m.–4:30 p.m.

■ **FEES:** Free access.

■ **ADDRESS:** Stewart B. McKinney NWR, P.O. Box 1030, Westbrook, CT 06498.

■ **TELEPHONE, FAX, AND E-MAIL:** 860/399-2513; fax: 860/399-2515; e-mail: R5RW_SBMNNWR@fws.gov

TOURING SALT MEADOW

■ **BY AUTOMOBILE:** Motor vehicles are not permitted.

■ **BY FOOT:** There are 2.5 miles of trails.

■ **BY BICYCLE:** Bicycles are not permitted.

■ **BY CANOE, KAYAK, OR BOAT:** Paddling the Menunketesuck River, which borders the refuge, is the only way to explore this portion of the refuge. Visitors may not enter the land portion of the refuge from the water. It is possible to navigate the river in motorboats up to 18 feet or so.

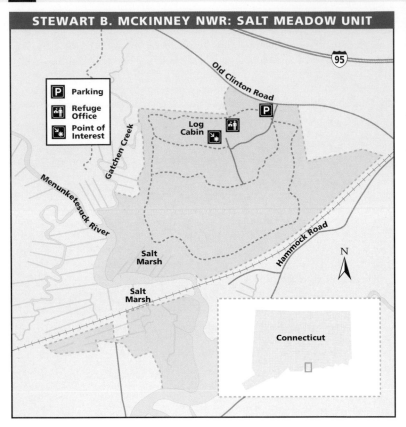

STEWART B. MCKINNEY NWR: SALT MEADOW UNIT

WHAT TO SEE

■ **LANDSCAPE AND CLIMATE** Situated at the critical juncture between land and sea, the tidal Menunketesuck River unites two worlds where its waters deposit the ever-eroding uplands. Those uplands are dotted with gneiss boulders, gifts of the ice sheet. A rich salt-marsh ecosystem is visible beyond the trunks of huge oaks and tulip trees. The air is often damp. When the relatively warm ocean air meets the cooler landmass, fog condenses and yields its moisture. Coastal southern New England experiences relatively mild fall and winter seasons compared with inland areas.

■ **PLANT LIFE**
Deciduous woodland Dominant trees are black birch, which invades bare ground; hickory, which usually associates with oaks; and black, red, and white oaks, some of which reach immense size here. Black tupelo (black gum), whose foliage turns red and orange in autumn, and tulip tree, a massive columnar species named for its large yellowish tuliplike flowers, thrive in damp soils.

A second level, the understory of small trees and shrubs, is populated by red maple, black cherry (its black bark is broken into small plates), and sassafras. The sassafras leaves (sometimes mitten shaped) exude a spicy, citric aroma when crushed. Look also for ironwood, which has a smooth, gray, sinewy trunk. Remnant red cedars (junipers, actually), which colonized this ground when it was pasture, have been shaded out. You will also find a few small American chestnuts, once dominant before the chestnut blight all but eliminated them from the landscape by the 1930s.

Below the trees are maple-leaf viburnum; arrowwood, so named because Native Americans made arrows from its long, straight branches; spicebush, whose oil-rich berries fuel thrushes and other migrants on their journeys; winged euonymus (its branches have paperlike ridges); highbush and early lowbush blueberries; and American hazelnut, a modest tree that produces nuts prized by wildlife.

Trees and shrubs are festooned with creeping vines that utilize them for support as they grow toward the sunlight. Very common here are poison ivy; greenbrier (shiny green heart-shaped leaves); Virginia creeper, which has five leaflets; oriental bittersweet and Chinese wisteria (both invasive exotics); and wild grape. The fruits of all these species are distributed by birds.

In spring, before the canopy steals the sunlight, the forest floor rejoices with wildflowers. The little twin heart-shaped leaves of the Canada mayflower virtually obscure the leaf litter. Solomon's seal and false Solomon's seal (the latter distinguished from the former by tiny white flowers along the end of the stem) flourish. Also common are striped (spotted) wintergreen, a characteristic plant of acidic oak woods that has fancy green and white foliage; partridgeberry, whose two small white flowers later develop into twin red berries; wild geranium, which has pinkish flowers; enchanter's nightshade; red baneberry; and meadow rue.

Wetter sites host a different floral collection, including skunk cabbage (the crushed foliage has a fetid odor); touch-me-not; and jack-in-the-pulpit, an almost comical caricature displaying a fingerlike "jack" beneath a leafy canopy.

Rich woodlands also display nonflowering mosses and ferns. The ferns include New York (common), lady, Christmas (evergreen), sensitive, and cinnamon. The last two require moist soils. Bracken is usually

Jack-in-the-pulpit

found in dry, sandy soils. New York fern is easy to identify: its fronds taper to a point at both ends.

Many alien species were planted near buildings on the former estate and include rows of tall European larch and Norway spruce, which produce 8-inch-long cones. Prickly branches and bright red berries identify Japanese barberry. Morrow honeysuckle produces red berries eaten by robins and other songbirds. Both of these exotic shrubs are invasive and difficult to eradicate.

Salt marsh The refuge is named for the salt marsh within which salt-meadow cordgrass, usually procumbent, is the dominant plant; it gives the marsh its characteristic "flattened" appearance. On slightly higher ground stands the taller salt-marsh cordgrass. Both represent the base of the food chain. Salt-marsh bulrush is also present.

Along the edges of the marsh, other plants adapted to saline soils are able to exist. Sea lavender, a small bushy plant, displays many tiny lilac blossoms in midsummer. American germander, or wood sage, a mint with purplish flowers, grows along the shore. Two woody shrubs, marsh elder and groundsel tree, delineate the high-tide line.

Fields Some fields, uncut for years, are filling up with black cherry, bayberry, Morrow honeysuckle, staghorn sumac (many birds eat the fuzzy red berries), winged (shining) sumac—which sports glistening green leaves—and alternate-leaf dogwood. An introduced species, *Multiflora rose,* was once widely planted for erosion control and as food and cover for wildlife. Mockingbirds love it.

In open meadows and brushy fields you will find tall sweet-scented joe-pye weed with its flat-topped clusters of pink flowers; striking orange-flowered butterfly weed (an aptly named milkweed); spotted Saint-John's-wort, which has star-shaped yellow blossoms; black-eyed Susan, the familiar garden plant, actually a midwestern native; and goldenrods.

■ ANIMAL LIFE

Birds Many species of waterfowl, shorebirds, and songbirds nest, feed, and rest at the Salt Meadow Unit of the Stewart B. McKinney NWR.

Nesting songbirds with southern affinities include the northern cardinal, Carolina wren, tufted titmouse (the only small gray bird with a crest), and red-bellied woodpecker. Look for the black-and-white "zebra-back" and the scarlet on the crown, but don't expect to see the subtle pinkish wash on its belly. The white-eyed vireo, unlike other vireos, has yellow irises and sings a sharp, rather unmusical "song." It prefers to skulk in brushy tangles and thickets.

Great egret, Milford Point Unit

Other woodland breeders abound. The red-eyed vireo sings even at midday in July. The emphatic *teacher, teacher, teacher* of the ovenbird, a ground-nesting warbler, resounds through the forest in spring. Watch and listen for the scarlet tanager, a gorgeous neotropical migrant; the American robin (the Connecticut state bird); wood thrush; and veery, a smallish, cinnamon-backed thrush.

In brushy tangles, listen for the gray catbird (one call is reminiscent of a cat's *meow*). The eastern towhee seems to say *drink your tea*. The sharp-shinned hawk, a small long-tailed and short-winged woodland raptor, preys on smaller birds. The largest winged predator in this ecosystem, the powerful great horned owl, dispatches prey as large as a striped skunk, apparently with impunity! Look for their cast-up pellets (regurgitated undigested material) under the big spruces.

In open expanses of the salt-marsh environment, look and listen for both American and fish crows; the latter's call is much more nasal. Double-crested cormorants dive for fish, while herons and egrets stalk or pursue them in the shallows. Red-winged blackbirds and the rakish belted kingfishers are part of the watery ensemble.

Mammals Cottontail rabbits nibble leafy and woody vegetation in brushy fields and woodland edges, ever alert for their ardent predators—red fox and coyote. Look for rabbit fur in scat left along the trail by foxes and coyotes. Small mounds of loose earth on the surface indicate the presence of tunneling eastern moles, little-known animals that feed on earthworms and insect larvae as they "swim" through the soil.

The most abundant mammal of the salt marshes, the muskrat, protected by luxuriant underfur and long, glossy guard hairs, stays dry and warm in its watery surroundings. Muskrats feed on a wide variety of plant and animal foods.

Reptiles and amphibians The red-backed salamander (some have gray rather than red backs) has been called the most abundant vertebrate in eastern woodlands. These slender amphibians, three-and-one-half inches long, spend the daylight hours under decaying logs and venture out in the cool of night in search of earthworms. If you uncover one, be sure to roll the log back to its original position.

Invertebrates Warm summer days are filled with the incessant, buzzy drone of dog day cicadas, plump insects that crawl up tree trunks after emerging from pupation in the ground. Male cicada song, produced by two organs on their abdomens, is one of the most familiar sounds during the dog days of late summer.

Brightly patterned butterflies sip nectar in sunny habitats where meadows are kept open by mowing. Butterfly weed and other nectar-rich plants lure the exquisite coral hairstreak, a small butterfly with red markings on brown underwings.

Close examination of the bare, sandy soil near the Visitor Center reveals the small conical pits of ant lions, voracious big-jawed insect larvae that lie in wait for hapless insects to blunder into their traps. After one to three years the larvae transform into damselfly-like adults.

ACTIVITIES

■ **CAMPING:** Not permitted; the nearest public campground is at Hammonasset Beach State Park in Madison.

■ **SWIMMING:** Not permitted on refuge property.

■ **WILDLIFE OBSERVATION:** Birds and butterflies in the woodlands and fields are among the most watchable of Salt Meadow's wildlife. The greatest avian activity occurs from early May through early July, when breeding birds are singing. Midsummer and late summer are opportune for observing butterflies and other insect life. The salt marshes are rich with life, but can be explored only

Coral hairstreak butterfly alighting on bright-flowered butterfly weed

in canoes or kayaks. The refuge does not supply boats; you may bring in your own canoe or kayak or rent one in Westbrook. U.S. Fish & Wildlife Service signs are posted where access is denied; trespassers risk being fined or ticketed.

■ **PHOTOGRAPHY:** Field flowers and their attendant butterflies are wonderful summer subjects. The old stone walls and fall foliage of the towering trees are photogenic. The foggy salt marsh at dawn rewards the early-bird photographer.

■ **HIKES AND WALKS:** Two and one-half miles of trails traverse woodlands and old fields over gently rolling terrain, with an elevation gain of 100 feet. The trail system, although very passable, is not marked and can be confusing even with a map. (A map kiosk is near the Visitor Center.) This is nonetheless an enjoyable place to walk, and future improvements will probably include better marking. You will enjoy resting at the stone slab picnic table in front of the Visitor Center.

■ **SEASONAL EVENTS:** None conducted at present.

■ **PUBLICATIONS:** None available at present.

Rachel Carson NWR
Wells, Maine

Wildlife viewing platform, Carson Trail, Upper Wells Division, Rachel Carson NWR

Lying like a string of pearls along 43 miles of coastline, the 10 divisions in this refuge protect some of Maine's most valuable and biologically productive coastal estuaries—tidal salt marshes as well as sandy beaches and pine oak woodlands—amid heavy residential and recreational development. The vibrant interface between wooded upland and salt marsh, broad sandy beaches, and a rocky inter-tidal zone beckons the naturalist. During the autumn migration, tidal Biddeford Pool lures countless shorebirds to its expansive mudflats, revealed twice daily by a falling tide. Given its rocky coastline, Maine has relatively few salt marshes, so the gems protected by this refuge are all the more valuable.

HISTORY

Established in 1966 as Coastal Maine NWR, the refuge was renamed in 1970 for pioneer environmentalist Rachel Carson, the renowned author whose 1962 exposé, *Silent Spring,* raised public awareness of the lasting consequences of pesticide use. Carson worked for the U.S. Fish & Wildlife Service from 1936 until 1952. This popular refuge comprises almost 5,000 acres and attracts 360,000 visitors annually. When acquisition is complete, it will span 7,435 acres.

GETTING THERE

From I-95 (Maine Turnpike), take Exit 2 and travel east on Rte. 9 to Rte. 1, then take Rte. 1 east (north) to where Rte. 9 splits from Rte. 1. Follow Rte. 9 for .6 mi.to refuge entrance on right. This is for Upper Wells Division, Headquarters, and Carson Trail.

To access wildlife observation areas in Wells, where much of the shoreline lies within the refuge, use three roads that cross open salt marsh east from Rte, 1: Mile Rd., Lower Landing Rd., and Drake's Island Rd. For Mile Rd., take Exit 2 and go east on Rtes. 9/109, then turn right (south) and drive 1.3 mi. to Mile Road on the left. To reach Lower Landing Rd., travel east (north) from Mile Rd. on Rte. 1 to Lower Landing Rd. on right, just beyond fire station; park on right at end of road. To reach Drake's Island Rd., continue heading east (north) on Rte. 1 from Lower Landing Rd. to Drake's Island Rd. on right, about 1 mi.

Biddeford Pool is about 27 mi. north of Kennebunkport. Here Rte. 208 bears east (right) off Rte. 9 and junctions with Fletcher's Neck. Turn left onto Fletcher's Neck and drive slightly less than 1 mi. to parking at the public beach lot on left, across from Hattie's Deli.

■ **SEASON:** Refuge open year-round. Carson Trail sometimes closed in winter because of icy conditions.

■ **HOURS:** Refuge open dawn to dusk. Headquarters open weekdays, 8 a.m. to 4:30 p.m.

■ **FEES:** Free access.

■ **ADDRESS:** Rachel Carson NWR, RR 2, Box 751, Wells, ME 04090.

■ **TELEPHONE, FAX, AND E-MAIL:** 207/646-9226; fax: 207/646-6554; e-mail: R5RW_RCNWR@fws

TOURING RACHEL CARSON NWR

■ **BY AUTOMOBILE:** Automobiles are not permitted beyond refuge parking areas.

■ **BY FOOT:** All visitor facilities are at headquarters; the 1-mile Carson Trail, at

Salt marsh, Rachel Carson NWR

headquarters, is a self-guiding loop. You may walk along Wells Beach at the end of Mile Rd. At Biddeford Pool, take the private path behind Hattie's Deli (ask for permission inside). Cross-country skiing is permitted on refuge trails.

■ **BY BICYCLE:** Bicycling on refuge trails is not permitted.

■ **BY CANOE, KAYAK, OR BOAT:** Branch Brook and the Mariland River, at headquarters, are both tributaries of the Little River, which flows into the Gulf of Maine (Atlantic Ocean) a short distance to the southeast; this tidal river system is navigable by canoe or kayak. Shallow Biddeford Pool, ringed by refuge property, is accessible by boat at high tide.

WHAT TO SEE

■ **LANDSCAPE AND CLIMATE** The southern Maine coast below Port Elizabeth contains many estuaries. It does not have the rocky headlands so stereotypical farther north. The Carson Trail traverses acidic pine oak woodlands perched at the edge of an extensive salt-marsh ecosystem. At one point along the trail, the ocean is visible beyond the broad expanse of tidal marsh (90 percent of the refuge is coastal wetlands). Broad, sandy beaches characterize the Wells area, where the intertidal zone below the strand is marked by rockweed-covered granite boulders.

Spring comes late to coastal Maine because of the cool easterly ocean breezes; as a corollary, autumn is mild and lingers while inland areas are experiencing their first snowfalls. Summers are relatively cool and very pleasant, and winters are far milder than in the inland areas farther south.

■ **PLANT LIFE**
Intertidal zone The intertidal environment at Wells Beach imposes hostile conditions for most plants, but some thrive. At low tide, rockweeds in abundance cling to granite boulders. Their holdfasts enable rockweeds to adhere to rocks and resist pounding waves. Some of these olive-green plants have gas-filled floats and provide vital habitat and cover for myriad creatures.
Dunes American beach grass is the characteristic dune grass along the northeast coast, and you will find it here in the dunes along with saltspray (*Rugosa*) rosebushes that display showy pink blossoms. Bayberry and beach plum, sporting inch-long dark blue fruit, provide a wildlife repast.
Pine-oak (transition) forest Carson Trail leads through uplands that hold white pine, eastern hemlock, and several oaks; decaying needles and leaves contribute to formation of its acidic soil. Some of the many stately white pines are imposing, and among the equally numerous black and red oaks are sizable red oak specimens. Distinguishing the two related oaks is not always easy, but compared to those of the red oak, black oak leaves are generally broader, have fewer points, and tend to be glossier above.

Red maple, which tolerates both wet and dry soils, grows here, as do the white and gray birch and the American beech. Gray-green leaflike lichens cover the gray trunks of the oaks; lichens are an indication of unpolluted air. The 6-inch princess pine, a clubmoss, pokes up from the forest floor.

Shrubs include lowbush blueberry, just 12 inches high, and the hobblebush, which has heart-shaped leaves, and wild raisin. Common, too, is alder buckthorn, a tall shrub with distinctly veined, shiny leaves. Beaked hazel forms interesting fruit—nuts covered by long, beak-shaped sheaths. The nuts, highly prized by mammals, do not remain long. Woody poison ivy vines cling to the trees with rootlike suckers; they produce whitish berries that wildlife eat.

The acid soils also provide excellent conditions for Canada mayflower, an indicator of maturing oak woods. Other late-spring bloomers include starflower (twin white blossoms, each with six or seven petals), Indian cucumber root (its edible tuber is pinkie-sized), pretty yellow-flowered Clintonia, bunchberry (a tiny dogwood with red berries), pink lady's slipper (a showy June orchid), and the ghostly white Indian pipes, a plant that has no green chlorophyll. Another parasite, green and up to 12 inches tall, is cowwheat; its modest snapdragon-like flowers are white and yellow. Forest nutrients are carried by groundwater to the salt marsh.

Boreal forest A regenerating boreal forest of fragrant balsam fir is present in the Goosefare Brook area, but this part of the refuge is off-limits to visitors.

Salt marsh Spartina grasses-both salt-meadow cordgrass and saltwater cordgrass—are the key plants in this ecosystem. The tall, smooth-stemmed grass growing adjacent to tidal creek banks is saltwater cordgrass; it actually initiates the creation of salt marsh by trapping silt with its extensive root system. Salt-meadow cord grass, or salt hay, is shorter and generally grows above mean-high-tide level. It is often prostrate, as if it had been blown over. Each produces up to 10 tons of organic matter per acre per year, as much as a fertile Iowa cornfield. Along the upland edge of the salt marsh you will find a third *Spartina*, freshwater cordgrass.

Seaside goldenrod borders the margins of tidal creeks. Sea lavender has a spindly shrublike growth form and shows off tiny lavender flowers in late summer. Glasswort, a small succulent salt-tolerant plant, has no leaves and turns red in late summer; it grows in shallow pools called salt pans.

Freshwater wetlands Along the edge of the salt marsh, where freshwater drains from adjacent uplands, common reed *(Phragmites)* flourishes. It outcompetes grasses such as cattails. Less familiar than grasses to most people are rushes and sedges, which superficially resemble them. Three-square, or chair-maker's, rush has small brown scaly flower clusters near the tip of one side of its triangular stem.

■ ANIMAL LIFE

Birds Because of the diversity of habitats, some 250 species have been recorded.

Great blue heron

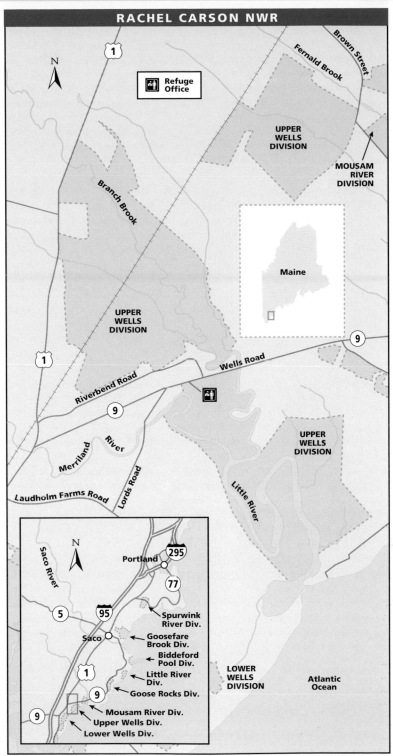

RACHEL CARSON NWR

N

Refuge Office

Brown Street

Fernald Brook

UPPER WELLS DIVISION

MOUSAM RIVER DIVISION

Branch Brook

Maine

UPPER WELLS DIVISION

9

Wells Road

Riverbend Road

9

Merriland River

Lords Road

Laudholm Farms Road

UPPER WELLS DIVISION

Little River

N

Saco River

Portland

295

77

5

95

Spurwink River Div.

Saco

Goosefare Brook Div.

Biddeford Pool Div.

1

Little River Div.

9

Goose Rocks Div.

9

Mousam River Div.

Upper Wells Div.

Lower Wells Div.

LOWER WELLS DIVISION

Atlantic Ocean

Shorebirds and waterfowl are among the most numerous and prominent families. In summer, look for the spotted sandpiper, brightly colored ruddy turnstone, and large willet, which displays bold flashes of white when it spreads its wings. In spring and autumn, migrant sandpipers and plovers feed and rest along the ocean beaches and on the salt-marsh mudflats at low tide.

Long-legged wading birds populate the salt marshes and shores, seeking fish, frogs, crabs, and worms. These include the great blue heron; snowy egret; perhaps the much larger great egret (yellow-orange bill); glossy ibis, whose long curved bill is especially designed to extract fiddler crabs from their burrows; and the black-crowned night heron. American black ducks nest in the tidal rivers and marshes, feeding on mud snails and other morsels.

Birds to watch for in saltwater are black guillemot, a member of the auk family, which is mostly white in winter; common loon (breeds on inland lakes); common eider (a few nest this far south, so watch for fuzzy ducklings with their brown mothers); and the fish-eating double-crested cormorant. Graceful common terns nest on islands offshore. Diving ducks such as common goldeneye, bufflehead, old-squaw, and red-breasted merganser winter here.

Hawk migration can be an exciting spectacle, especially along the coast in fall when winds are right. Northwest winds in late September and early October send thousands of broad-winged and sharp-shinned hawks southward. Shorebird-eating falcons, merlin and peregrine, follow their food species as far as Central America and even northern South America.

Mammals Harbor seals, the most common seals along this coast, now breed on rocky offshore islets. Dozens of seals sometimes haul out on rocks 100 yards off Wells Beach at low tide. The seals, both young and 250-pound adults, are of various colors.

Aquatic mammals occupying the salt-marsh zone include fish-eating river otters. In the freshwater marshes muskrats build conical lodges of mud and vegetation (generally cattails). The omnivorous raccoons are especially fond of ribbed mussels, crabs, and other aquatic fare that they find along the edges of the salt marsh.

Porcupines have few natural enemies because of their formidable covering of barbed quills. Vehicles kill many, however, as they lumber across roadways in the glare of headlights. Porcupines feast on the inner bark of trees.

Reptiles and amphibians Red-backed salamanders are common in the woodlands, spending the daylight hours under fallen trees. If you uncover one by rolling a log, return the log to its original position.

Fishes Tidal estuaries are nurseries for many species of shellfish and finfish. During a portion of their life cycles, commercially important species such as flounder, bluefish, and striped bass all depend on this protected and nutrient-rich environment. Among the smaller, less conspicuous salt-marsh fish, the mummichog grows to about 3 inches in length and is marked by dark vertical stripes.

Invertebrates On rocks at low tide, you will find clumps of edible blue mussels, periwinkles grazing algae from the rocks, and the tortoiseshell limpet, which carries a shield-shaped shell and clings tenaciously to rocks. Slipper or boat shells are snails that have one shell equipped with a "deck." They often cling to each other in a stack, with the larger females on the bottom, males on top, and hermaphrodites (undergoing sexual change) between.

The three-quarter-inch conical dog whelk, a major predator of mussels, bores a round hole through its prey's shell, then sucks out and digests the contents. Barnacles, armored against the power of the surf, cover the rocks exposed by a falling tide. When inundated, they kick minute floating creatures into their mouths with their feathery "feet." Look for comical hermit crabs in tide pools left by the receding tide. Small crabs seem to prefer dog-whelk shells for homes and use their pincers to close off the shell's entrance when frightened.

Ribbed mussels anchor themselves to cordgrass stems with strong threads at the peaty fringe of the salt marshes, where they provide sustenance for predators.

Dragonflies patrol the skies for salt-marsh mosquitoes and other unwary prey, while tiny female sand flies ("no-see-ums") deliver painful bites to anyone who ventures into their salt-marsh domain, especially at dusk.

ACTIVITIES

■ **SWIMMING AND CAMPING:** Wells Beach, an excellent public beach, is crowded in summer. Camping is not permitted on the refuge. The many nearby private campgrounds include four in Wells.

■ **WILDLIFE OBSERVATION:** Access to salt marshes is limited mostly to viewing from public roadways. Several roads between Rte. 1 and the beach area

Harbor seals congregating on Atlantic coastal beach

around Wells provide opportunities for viewing herons, egrets, ducks, and shorebirds. Biddeford Pool, accessible via a trail on private property, is one of the finest shorebirding spots in southern Maine, especially on a low or falling tide from July to September.

Public beaches permit access to the ocean shores, but plan to arrive early to see shorebirds in late summer. Scan the offshore rocks for harbor seals and the water for sea ducks and, during migration, loons.

Bird feeders are stocked year-round at headquarters. A refuge bird checklist is available at the information board. Watch for the buglike ruby-throated hummingbird at sugar water feeders and blooming plants from May to August. Clouds of tree swallows feed over the marshes in late summer, fattening up before departing.

HUNTING AND FISHING A permit for hunting on the refuge is required. Hunting is allowed on seven of 10 divisions; seasons and game that is allowed to be hunted change from year to year. Current regulations and maps showing hunting areas are available at the refuge office. For information on current license requirements, seasons, and bag limits, consult the refuge office.

Very limited areas will be open in the near future for fishing; consult refuge staff for current regulations.

■ **PHOTOGRAPHY:** Birds and seals make fine telephoto subjects. The broad expanses of marsh and beach environments in morning light have great visual appeal. Most environments are open and well lit. At the other end of the spectrum: intimate close-ups of the hairstreak butterfly or hermit crab.

■ **HIKES AND WALKS:** The 1-mile-loop Carson Trail, the only developed footpath, is level and hard-packed, well chipped, and graveled and thus wheelchair-accessible. A self-guiding leaflet to this pleasant walk, available at the trailhead, provides interesting insight into the interplay between upland, salt marsh, and ocean. Picnic tables are available; pack out all trash. An accessible chemical toilet is also present. The trail may be closed during icy conditions.

A walk on Wells Beach, especially at low tide, provides the only real way to explore the rich and fascinating intertidal environment (watch your footing on the slippery rockweed-covered granite boulders).

■ **SEASONAL EVENTS:** Contact the refuge Visitor Center for program information.

Scarborough Marsh Nature Center, operated by the Maine Audubon Society, adjoins 3,000-acre Scarborough Marsh, which is owned by the Maine Department of Inland Fisheries & Wildlife as part of the Scarborough Wildlife Management Area. The center, on Pine Point Rd., conducts public programs, including canoe tours and wildflower and dawn bird walks from late June to early September (207/883-5100).

■ **PUBLICATIONS:** Two leaflets are available from refuge headquarters: "Carson Trail Guide" and "Birds of Rachel Carson National Wildlife Refuge."

Moosehorn NWR
Baring and Dennysville, Maine

Beaver lodge in a pond, Moosehorn NWR

The rolling land of northeast Maine is laced with streams and dotted with lakes, bogs, swamps, and marshes, a mosaic of habitats for a vast array of wildlife. In places, an almost impenetrable growth of young spruces creates a damp, dark boreal forest. In much of the remainder of the refuge, a regenerating forest dominated by aspen, red maple, birch, spruce, and balsam fir clothes a landscape in the process of reverting to its original wild state.

HISTORY

Early European settlers farmed on present-day refuge lands. The refuge was established in 1937 to provide sanctuary and breeding habitat for migratory birds and other wildlife. The two units of land that make up Moosehorn total 24,446 acres; nearly 7,500 acres are part of the National Wilderness Preservation System. These congressionally designated lands are granted special protection that insures preservation of their wilderness qualities. (None of the refuge, however, contains virgin forest.) More than 50,000 people visit the refuge each year.

GETTING THERE

For refuge headquarters (Baring Unit), drive north on Rte. 1 to Rte. 214 at West Pembroke. Turn left and travel northwest to Charlotte Rd. (about 5 mi.). Turn right (note refuge sign) and then left; travel northward on Charlotte Rd. a distance of about 7.5 mi. Headquarters is on Headquarters Rd., a left turn off Charlotte Rd. The southwestern portion of the Baring Unit is accessible from Rte. 191, north of Meddybemps.

The Edmunds Unit lies about 12 mi. south of the Baring Unit along Rte. 1. From Whiting, at junction of Rtes. 1 and 189, take Rte. 1 north for about 5.5 mi. to several small parking areas on left.

■ **SEASON:** Refuge open year-round.

■ **HOURS:** Refuge open dawn to dusk; Visitor Center open Mon.–Fri., 7:30 a.m.–4 p.m.

■ **FEES:** Free access; donation box at headquarters.

■ **ADDRESS:** Moosehorn NWR, RR1, Box 202, Suite 1, Baring, ME 04694-9703.

■ **TELEPHONE, FAX, AND E-MAIL:** Refuge headquarters: 207-454-7161; fax: 207-454-2550; e-mail: R5RW_MHNWR@fws.gov

TOURING MOOSEHORN

■ **BY AUTOMOBILE:** Public highways offer wildlife viewing opportunities; pull all the way off the road so as not to impede traffic. Small parking areas or turnouts are situated along highways, generally at junctions with former logging roads. Vehicles are not allowed on logging roads or trails (except snowmobiles in winter).

■ **BY FOOT:** More than 50 miles of graveled former logging roads and footpaths invite exploration. Chemical toilets, but no picnic tables, are at headquarters. Cross-country skiing and snowshoeing are also permitted.

■ **BY BICYCLE:** Many miles of old logging roads are excellent for mountain biking; rentals available in Pembroke. Mountain bikes are not permitted off-road or in designated wilderness areas.

■ **BY CANOE, KAYAK, OR BOAT:** Boat access (off Rte. 191) is provided at Bearce Lake in the designated wilderness of the Baring Unit. In keeping with its wilderness mandate, no motors are allowed. You can canoe Vose Pond in the northeastern portion of the Baring Unit. You can also boat on Meddybemps Lake, bordering the Baring Unit.

Portions of the Edmunds Unit border Cobscook Bay; the bay provides fine canoeing and kayaking. It is possible to canoe many other flowages, but frequent portaging is necessary.

WHAT TO SEE

■ **LANDSCAPE AND CLIMATE** What is now refuge was once heavily glaciated; sand and gravel are the legacy of retreating ice. Outcrops of granite and other hard rock abound, and deep gouges incised in the bedrock by the advancing ice are still visble. The Edmunds Unit has several miles of saltwater shoreline where some of the highest tides (24 to 28 feet) in the lower 48 states occur twice daily.

Summers are generally cool and moist; winters are harsh with abundant snowfall. Summer mornings are often foggy, but clearing usually occurs by mid- to late morning.

■ PLANT LIFE

Boreal forest Spruce and fir predominate in these cool, damp woodlands. White spruce can be distinguished from red spruce by white spruce's blue-green (not yellowish-green) needles. Set among the spruces are stands of balsam fir, a fragrant fir with a seductive perfume. Fir needles are soft to the touch; those of spruce are sharp and prickly.

Lichens cover nearly every surface. An especially conspicuous type is lung lobaria; its pitted and ribbed texture is reminiscent of that organ. Relying on airborne dust minerals for food and precipitation for drink, lichens thrive in unpolluted air; their extravagance is a favorable clue to the area's air quality.

Few plants can tolerate the darkness and acidic conditions beneath dense evergreens. Among the few that do are bunchberry, which grows in dappled sun.

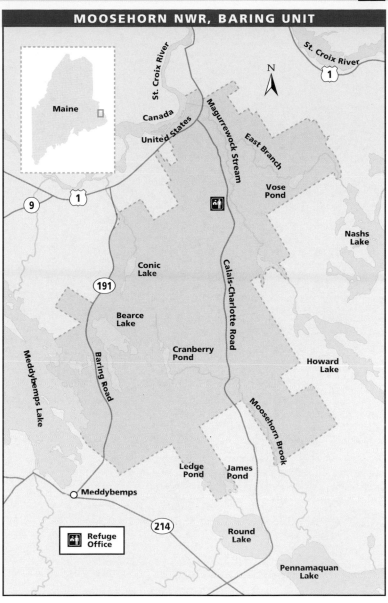

MOOSEHORN NWR, BARING UNIT

This tiny dogwood, no more than 6 inches tall, has six parallel-veined leaves in a whorl and elegant white blossoms that become scarlet berries. Canada mayflower's frothy white flowers grace the coniferous woods in early summer.

Early-summer woodlands of the Baring Unit offer Clintonia, a true lily that has two to four tongue-shaped leaves and nodding yellow flowers. Starflower has five to nine tapered light-green leaves that form a whorl, whereas creeping twinflower has small rounded and paired dark evergreen leaves.

Northern hardwood forest Maples, birches, beech, and some evergreens characterize this forest. Yellow birch is a dominant, its bark brassy and metallic when young. American beech, distinguished by smooth, light gray skin and

MOOSEHORN NWR, EDMUNDS UNIT

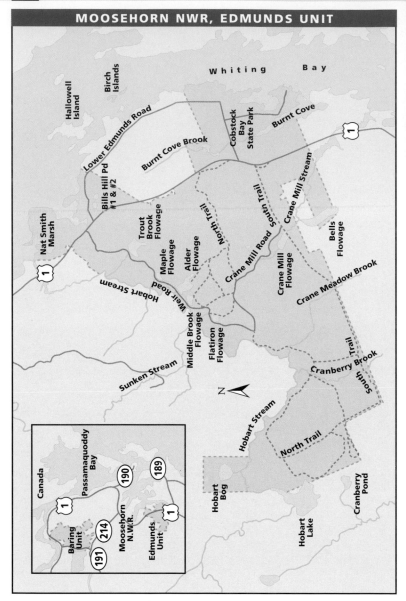

papery leaves, thrives only in moist, rich woodlands. Below the canopy, striped maple shows striated green and white bark. The deep-green needles of American yew resemble hemlock or fir, but this evergreen species never attains tree height in the moist woods where it grows. Club mosses, resembling small evergreen trees on the damp forest floor, date back 300 million years; they spread by shallow runners and reproduce by spores.

Beaver flowages The brilliant cardinal flower blooms in August along stream and pond banks, including Hobart Stream (Edmunds Unit). Here, too, dwells poisonous water hemlock, whose floral head resembles Queen Anne's lace. Blue flag blossoms in early summer, and by late summer has formed plump green seed pods. Turtlehead—its twin white flowers resemble its reptilian namesake—provides leafy forage for Baltimore butterfly caterpillars. Boneset, a hairy plant with clasping leaves, was once valued for its reputed medicinal qualities. The tubular orange flowers of jewel-weed, or spotted touch-me-not, attract hummingbirds; when ripe, the edible seeds explode from the pod on contact.

In still water, look for water plantain with its tiny blossoms at the end of a treelike stalk. Another emergent that prefers ponds is bur reed. Flowers of this cattail-like plant are globular and white and become spiny green globes. The large triangular leaves of pickerel-weed cluster along the banks and flank a blue flower spike in early summer. Water smartweed has two distinct forms; the aquatic form puts out a cluster of small pink blossoms that rise two inches above the water's surface.

Beaver in its aquatic habitat

Beavers munch on succulent roots of bullhead lily in summer, and bladder-wort's yellow pealike flowers poke out from beaver ponds. Underwater, tiny bladders capture minute creatures when they trigger the bladder by bumping into it—an ingenious way to get nitrogen, often lacking in this acidic environment. Water horsetail grows to 3 feet or more in standing water of many flowages; its jointed stems contain abrasive silica, hence its nickname "scouring rush."

Marshes Cattails, ubiquitous members of the grass family, look something akin to plump hot dogs on long sticks. They grow from a thick, starchy tuber favored by muskrats, who also utilize the leaves to construct their lodges. Spread by runners, cattails colonize large areas in shallow marshes, creating cover and nesting sites for many birds.

Bogs Atlantic white-cedar, with flattened needles and conical form, grows in thick stands that shelter deer herds in winter. Below, the sphagnum moss contains large dead cells able to hold 250 times the plant's weight in water. In early summer the water arum, or wild calla, which has heart-shaped leaves, unfurls a lovely flower similar to the florist's calla lily. In wet meadows, cotton grass (not a true grass), also known as bog cotton, waves a white or tawny tuft at the tip of its single stem.

The wetland mosaic includes sweet gale, whose aromatic leaves are covered by resin dots underneath; mountain holly, with bristle-tipped leaves; and leatherleaf. Leatherleaf's thickened leaves retard water loss; note the scaly, rusty undersides. In spring white bell-shaped flowers resemble those of blueberry, another member of the heath family. Moosehorn's smallest shrub, mountain cranberry, a creeping plant, has the small leathery evergreen leaves of other cranberries, but with one notable difference: its leaves are dotted with minute black spots below.

Blueberry barrens Active management has created many acres of "blueberry barrens" that attract people and wildlife in August. In especially productive lowbush blueberry fields near headquarters, visitors lugging five-gallon buckets full of fruit are a regular sight. These same fields enable male American woodcocks to perform spring courtship rituals; they spiral into the air, circle, and plunge to the earth, calling out.

One of the most eye-catching summer flowers, the pink and aptly named fireweed, is abundant in recently cleared and burned areas.

■ ANIMAL LIFE

Birds More than 215 species of birds have been identified; 130 have bred, including 23 species of colorful wood warblers, "butterflies of the bird world." Evergreen forest warblers include the black, yellow, and white magnolia; yellow-rumped; the lovely bay-breasted; the fiery orange, black, and white Blackburnian; the black-necklaced Canada; black-throated green; and handsome northern parula.

In mixed woodlands, listen and watch for the gray and white Tennessee warbler, black-throated blue, and ovenbird—it resembles a small thrush and sings an emphatic, ringing *teacher, teacher, teacher.* In shrubby fields and forest edges, look for the white-spectacled, olive-backed, and yellow-throated Nashville warbler and the tail-wagging palm warbler. Thrushes, the rusty, spot-breasted, ground-nesting birds of rich woods, are among the world's most accomplished singers; listen for the veery's flutelike, descending phrases and the ethereal tones of the hermit thrush.

Even more animated than warblers are two of our smallest birds—ruby-crowned and golden-crowned kinglets. These bundles of energy search evergreen needles for adult insects, larvae, and eggs. Listen carefully for a northern specialty, boreal chickadee. Usually recognized first by its nasal calls, this brown-capped bird seems shyer than its familiar cousin. Give every big black bird a second look; the deep guttural croak of the common raven is unmistakable. One of the prettier singers of the north woods is the raspberry-colored (male) purple finch; the similar house finch, found near refuge buildings, is not native to the Northeast.

A special treat for birders in boreal wetlands, the olive-sided flycatcher has a big head and fluffy white patches on its lower back. Rarer to spot are one of the three-toed woodpeckers—the black-backed woodpecker, an uncommon resident. Black-backs scale away the outer bark of standing dead trees in search of insect larvae.

Most refuge drainages have been altered for waterfowl; some ponds provide nesting habitat for American black, wood, and ring-

AMERICAN WOODCOCK The American woodcock, or "timber doodle," is the object of considerable management activity at Moosehorn. These chunky shorebirds frequent refuge alder swamps by day and court in fields kept open by cutting and burning at dusk; forests are managed on a 40-year rotation for their benefit. Biologists trap woodcocks in wire cages set in muddy spots in the woods where the reclusive birds probe for earthworms with their long, flexible-tipped beaks. Birds are guided into the trap along a "drift fence" and banded. You may happen upon such traps in your travels through the refuge. The average summer population is 1,800 birds, and more than 3,000 are present during migrations.

necked ducks, blue-winged teal, and hooded merganser. Wood ducks and mergansers nest in big nest boxes. Common loons breed on secluded lakes; their haunting calls are emblematic of the north woods. Marshes are home to little pied-billed grebes, sometimes called hell-divers because of their prowess in underwater travel. Cattail marshes provide food and cover for the cryptically colored American bittern, a consummate marsh dweller. A resident of northern bogs, Lincoln's sparrow resembles the song sparrow, but shows finer breast streaking.

Ospreys nest on platforms in Magurrewock Marsh. They have white heads, with brown bands through their eyes; their tails are brown. In May this area is great for spotting bald eagles. Only adult eagles, at least five years old, have all-white heads and tails. The most imposing and powerful woodland hawk, the gray-backed northern goshawk, pursues prey as large as grouse.

Mammals Thirty-nine species of mammals have been recorded. Among the most common but seldom seen is the masked shrew, no bigger than your little finger. Shrews are carnivorous and known for their rapacious appetites. The related moles, insect eaters with a keen sense of smell and touch, spend even more time underground, searching for earthworms. Hairy-tailed moles inhabit refuge woodlands, while the peculiar star-nosed moles prefer damp soils.

Porcupines feed on the inner bark of trees and succulent herbs and fruits. Rather nearsighted, they rely on a keen sense of smell and a prickly coat for protection.

Beavers modify their surroundings to suit their mode of life. Dozens of beaver ponds, resulting from streams dammed with mud and sticks, are wonderful wildlife habitat. Beavers also construct lodges from the same materials. They eat succulent vegetation in summer and inner bark during leaner times in winter. Muskrats build lodges, too, albeit much smaller versions, using mud and cattails. River otters eat fish almost exclusively. These big weasels are more common than sightings would indicate. Mink, their smaller cousins, are also numerous.

A well-camouflaged American woodcock probes for earthworms in the leaves.

Moose do utilize refuge lands, especially wetlands and regenerating forests during the summer calving season, but you will probably find only their 6-inch tracks—these animals can be solitary and elusive. White-tailed deer, elegant browsers that frequent meadows at dawn and dusk, are seen much more often. The snowshoe hare, with its oversized hind feet, is white in winter and brown in summer; these varying hares are a staple in the diet of the stealthy bobcat.

Red fox and coyote rely less on stealth. Coyotes prey on rodents and hares. Their scat is composed of hair and bones. Both also consume carrion, fruit, and whatever else they chance upon.

The largest predator, actually an omnivore, is the black bear. An average-sized adult male weighs 300 pounds. Blueberry fields are irresistible to bears (and people, for that matter). Keep a good distance away from any bears you see. The saltwater environment of the Edmunds Unit is home to harbor seals; watch them poke their heads out of the water or bask on an offshore rock.

Reptiles and amphibians Northern water snake and eastern garter are found near the refuge's 55 water bodies, where they feed on fish, frogs, and insects. A bit of searching should turn up bull, green, leopard, pickerel, and wood frogs. Look for the bull and the similar green in the standing or sluggish waters of beaver ponds. Leopard and the related pickerel frog (which has rectangular rather than oval dark blotches on the back) sometimes wander far from water. Wood frogs must deposit their eggs in ephemeral woodland vernal pools.

Leopard frog

Both tree frogs are hard to spot. The larger gray tree frog, at the northern edge of its range here, can adjust its coloration to blend in with the surface it is on. This one-and-a-half-inch frog is bright orange below. Spring peepers, like their larger relatives, have adhesive disks at the ends of their toes. Spring wetlands ring with a chorus of these tiny insect-eaters.

Vernal pools are also vital to the reproductive success of blue-spotted salamanders. During daylight they remain moist and safe beneath logs. The red-spotted newt, an aquatic salamander of beaver ponds, is more familiar as the terrestrial red eft.

Fishes Thirty-three species have been documented. The vast network of cold, clear oxygen-rich streams that are part of the Gulf of Maine ecosystem harbors native brook trout. Beaver ponds and human-created water bodies, such as Meddybemps Lake, hold large populations of yellow perch and game fish such as smallmouth bass and pickerel. These predators feed on the many small species of dace and shiner.

Native Atlantic salmon populations have been declining in the Dennys and St. Croix river watersheds. Refuge management is striving to protect the watershed to help ensure good water quality. The decline of salmon has been due in part to wholesale damming of their spawning rivers, as well as the fouling of streams from logging and farming; pesticides may have played a role as well.

Invertebrates In summer, butterflies abound; an unusual one is the common branded skipper—which is not at all "common" here. Skipper caterpillars feed on

Common loons

grasses, and this species occurs in openings within the boreal forest. Another uncommon species is the handsome Appalachian brown that frequents brushy marshes; its larvae feed on sedges. This pinkish-brown creature displays 16 eye-spots on the undersides of its wings.

Obvious, too, are predaceous dragonflies; their voracious larvae prowl ponds. After crawling upon a plant stem and emerging as a clear-winged aerial hunter, dragonflies, with wraparound compound eyes, fly sorties after insects. Whirligig beetles often form aggregations on the surface of swamps or ponds. These ebony predators have eyes that see both above and below the surface as they whirl about, supported by the water's surface tension.

Tiger beetles are fast, agile, long-legged hunters encountered on roads and trails. Of more practical interest are biting insects. Deerflies (spotted wings) often make a nuisance of themselves; a hat is a must in summer. Mosquitoes can be bothersome, especially at dawn and dusk.

ACTIVITIES

■ **SWIMMING AND CAMPING:** Refuge waters are not suitable for swimming. Camping is not permitted; camp at Cobscook Bay State Park, adjacent to the Edmunds Unit off Rte. 1 in Whiting.

■ **WILDLIFE OBSERVATION:** To view nesting ospreys and eagles, visit Magurrewock Marsh (Baring Unit), near where Rte. 1 and Charlotte Rd. intersect; sometimes two nests holding chicks are visible from the road in midsummer. Eagles also frequent tidal waters of the Edmunds Unit. For the courting male woodcock, almost any clearing (mid-April to mid-May) at dusk will do. Check old apple orchards for porcupines and black bears in autumn. Deer are fairly easy to spot along refuge roads, especially at dawn and dusk.

For boreal chickadees, black-backed woodpeckers, gray jays, and spruce grouse, the second-growth spruce and fir woodlands of South Trail in the Edmunds Unit and the area near Snare Meadow in the Baring Unit are best. Visitors may accompany biologists on waterfowl- and woodcock-banding operations; check in advance with the refuge office.

■ **PHOTOGRAPHY:** The Edmunds Unit has fewer clearcuts near roads and trails, and a vibrant growth of young spruce and balsam fir engenders a lovely, fragrant setting.

(These clearcuts are not logging as such. Wildlife management creates block clearcuts in order to set in motion early successional habitats for creatures such as American woodcock. These habitats are also used by moose and white-tailed deer for browsing and some songbirds for feeding and nesting. Management leaves den trees standing.)

Capturing nesting ospreys and bald eagles is an enjoyable challenge. High-speed film is imperative in shaded woodlands.

■ **HIKES AND WALKS:** The Edmunds Unit offers wonderful woodland and wetland jaunts; you may walk all day without encountering another soul! Some trails in designated wilderness areas are overgrown and sparsely blazed; check with refuge staff before setting off. Failure to do so may result in your getting lost. A good trail map and compass are also recommended.

Bears are quite common; a visitor has a 30 percent chance of encountering one, especially early and late in the day. They are generally shy, retiring creatures. If you see a bear, make a lot of noise, and never come between a sow and her cubs.

HUNTING AND FISHING Hunting of **white-tailed deer** is permitted only in November, with both bows and firearms. Since 1954, controlled hunting has gradually brought the herd into desirable balance with the food supply, according to refuge biologists. Each year about 25 deer are taken.

Fishing is allowed only during the waterfowl breeding season. This usually lasts from July until September; call the refuge for exact dates. Many refuge streams and ponds are open to fishing, and boat access is provided at Bearce Lake (no motors) and Vose Pond, both in the Baring Unit. Numerous public fishing areas have been designated and posted along refuge roads. Species sought are **brook trout, smallmouth bass, pickerel,** and **yellow perch.** Ice fishing is also popular. **Pickerel** and **leopard frogs** may be collected for bait in summer meadows, an activity known as "frog picking."

Three short, easy self-guiding trails originate at headquarters—Woodcock Trail (.4 mile and wheelchair-accessible), Nature Trail (.8 mile), and the 1.5-mile Marsh Loop Trail.

■ **SEASONAL EVENTS:** None currently offered.

■ **PUBLICATIONS:** Three leaflets are available from headquarters: "Moosehorn National Wildlife Refuge," "Mammals of Moosehorn National Wildlife Refuge," and "Birds, Moosehorn National Wildlife Refuge."

Petit Manan NWR
Steuben, Maine

Rugged and rocky coastline skirting Petit Manan NWR

North of Portland, the majestic Maine coastline becomes ever more rugged and dramatic. Granite headlands, clothed in stunted spruce, gnarled jack pine, blueberry, and sheep laurel, thrust boldly out to the sea. Here, at land's end, sea air mingles with the evocative perfume of balsam fir. It's been said that Petit Manan is what Acadia National Park once was, long before Acadia became a popular destination for some 1 million visitors annually. Petit Manan offers a solitude that is hard to find at the better-known coastal locations. Indeed, on many days, you may be the only visitor in the refuge.

HISTORY

The Abenaki lived along this coast, fishing and hunting big game, furbearers, and birds. Europeans arrived as the 16th century ended, drawn by the resources of the forest and the bounty of the sea. By 1800, many of the larger islands were inhabited, at least seasonally. Two boasted schools and stores that supported fishermen and farmers who harvested hay and grazed sheep.

The refuge's name is a corruption of Mun-a-nook, a Maliseet-Passamaquoddy-Penobscot Indian phrase meaning "the island" or "island place." "Petit" separates this island from the much larger Grand Manan off New Brunswick.

The 6,800-acre refuge, visited by more than 40,000 people each year, was established in 1974 through land transfer and purchase, with help from the Coast Guard, The Nature Conservancy, and private individuals. In all, the refuge embraces 31 islands along 150 miles of coastline and has been expanded on the mainland, north of the peninsula.

Petit Manan manages four satellite island refuges: Seal Island (65 acres), used from World War II until 1952 as a bombing and shelling target; Franklin Island (a two-island complex totaling 20 acres); Cross Island (six islands comprising 1,355 acres); and Pond Island, a 10-acre island in the mouth of the Kennebec River near Popham Beach.

GETTING THERE

Take Rte. 1 about 3 mi. east of Steuben, to Pigeon Hill Rd. on the right (no refuge sign). Follow it for about 5 mi. to a small parking area on the right.

■ **SEASON:** Refuge open year-round. Refuge islands, except Bois Bubert, Halifax, and Cross, closed April-Aug. Seal Island is always closed because of danger from unexploded ordnance.

■ **HOURS:** Refuge open sunrise to sunset.

■ **FEES:** Free access.

■ **ADDRESS:** Petit Manan NWR, P.O. Box 279, Milbridge, ME 04658.

■ **TELEPHONE, FAX, AND E-MAIL:** 207/546-2124; fax: 207/546-7805; e-mail: R5RW_PMNWR@fws.gov

TOURING PETIT MANAN

■ **BY AUTOMOBILE:** Motor vehicles not permitted beyond the parking areas.

■ **BY FOOT:** Two hiking trails totaling 4 miles traverse Petit Manan Point. Visitors must remain on trails. No toilet or picnic facilities exist.

■ **BY BICYCLE:** Not permitted on refuge trails.

■ **BY CANOE, KAYAK, OR BOAT:** Island landings can be hazardous because of tides, currents, and weather conditions. Consult refuge staff before attempting to visit any island unit.

Two operators lead tours to Petit Manan Island to see Atlantic puffins: Acadian Whale Watcher and Sea Bird Companies; Bar Harbor, ME. Phone: 800/421-3307, 800/247-3794, 207/285-2025, 207/288-9794, or 207/288-9776. To get to the Golden Anchor Pier, take Rte. 3 (Eden St.) north from Bar Harbor to Regency Holiday Inn Marina on right, just north of Bluenose Ferry terminal. Bar Harbor Whale Watch Company, Bar Harbor, ME. Phone: 207/288-2386.

WHAT TO SEE

■ **LANDSCAPE AND CLIMATE** Tough granite bedrock and glacial debris combined to create soil best tolerated by sharp-needled spruces, low thickets of blueberry, and other acid-adapted plants. The cold Labrador Current, originating in the Canadian Arctic, keeps the Gulf of Maine as far south as Cape Cod Bay cool year-round. Spring arrives late. Summers are quite comfortable, with dense morning fog (a foghorn sounds every 30 seconds). Autumn is relatively mild, with maples and birches producing gaudy companion colors to the steadfast greens of conifers. Winter is frigid and snowbound.

■ PLANT LIFE

Boreal forest Trees are stunted because of the brief growing season and scant soils. You will find damp, boggy pockets where big Atlantic white cedar, red maple, and fragrant balsam fir flourish. Balsam fir produces deep shade, causing its own lower branches to die as the stand thickens. In contrast, jack pine requires fire to open its cones. White spruce, tall and stately, and red spruce, distinguished from white spruce by hairy branches (you may need a magnifying lens to see the hairs), crown the uplands.

The dead lower branches of spruces are festooned with pale green beard lichens; reindeer lichen blanket open ground. Moisture transforms the stiff combination of fungus and algae into a soft, spongy mass. Some woodland rocks are

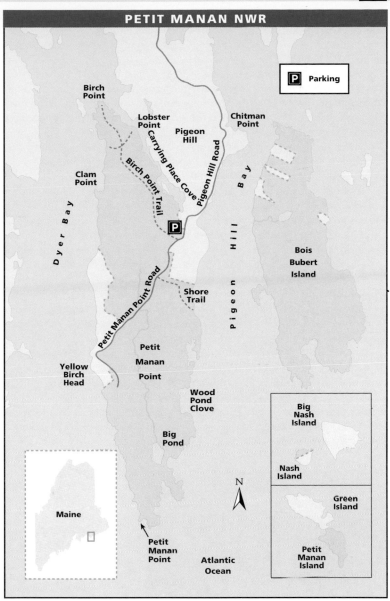

PETIT MANAN NWR

topped by lichen troops of red-capped British soldiers, or green goblet-shaped pixie cups, 1 inch tall. Clinging to damp tree roots are liverworts, which have no true leaves and reproduce by spores.

Low-growing bunchberry carpets the forest floor, its clusters of scarlet berries brightening the scene. Sprinkled about are the Canada mayflower; wild sarsaparilla (from the roots of which a substitute for sarsaparilla was concocted); starflower; and waxy white parasitic Indian pipes. At Birch Point a tiny mat-producing evergreen plant, black crowberry, develops fruit in late summer that is readily eaten by grouse and other birds. Look for the plant's tiny needles on the granite rocks, along with the red fruits of cranberries.

Among the evergreens are mixed broad-leaved species: red maple; picturesque white birch, some of which are very large; gray birch (distinguished from white birch by bark that peels less and is grayish on older specimens); mountain ash; and quaking aspen. Graceful cinnamon fern, which owes its name to the tall, bright russet fertile fronds, thrives in shaded wet woods.

Bogs Signature shrubs of cool acidic bogs include the two-foot-tall sheep laurel, which offers pretty pink flowers in early summer; Labrador tea, an unusual plant whose thick leathery leaves are covered by brown fuzz underneath to reduce water loss; American yew, a low-growing evergreen with flattened dark green needles and fleshy, translucent fruits; northern mountain cranberry; and aromatic sweet gale. The Rhodora azalea's blunt-tipped leaves and lovely purplish flowers bloom in spring and early summer. Tamarack, or larch, the deciduous conifer, is also common. Sphagnum moss carpets boggy pockets, and round-leaved sundew employs sticky leaves to entrap insects and then slowly digest them.

Fields Lowbush blueberry covers many acres; the sweet fruit delights berry pickers in early August. Management burns blueberry fields on a three-year rotation to keep them from becoming forest. This also provides food for deer and grouse and courting areas for woodcocks. Fields are also home to fireweed, sporting tall spikes of delicate pink flowers in summer; multiflowered goldenrods; and white lettuce. After fires, thorny red raspberry, creeping dewberry (which has white flowers), and steeplebush and its relative meadowsweet form thick growths. Other pioneers include felted willow (actually more of a shrub than a tree) and the aptly named fire or pin cherry.

Showy purple-flowered New York aster prospers along woodland edges together with sweet-scented bayberry, mountain alder, prickly gooseberry, nannyberry (a viburnum), and mountain holly, which, like other hollies, sports coral-red berries.

Rocky shore Olive and yellow-green rockweeds of several species obscure the granite boulders. Attached with tenacious holdfasts rather than roots, they prevail in the face of pounding surf, kept afloat by gas-filled bladders. At low tide, many creatures seek shelter among the wet fronds. In rock crevices, seaside plantain, a native, prevails; its thin, fleshy leaves are unlike those of the alien variety. Beach pea, the dune plant, seems a bit out of place here, but it makes do in the scant soil.

Salt marsh Familiar salt-marsh grasses of the coastline farther south, salt-meadow cordgrass and the taller saltwater cordgrass, stand in the narrow intertidal zone at the end of the Hollingsworth Memorial Trail. Black grass, actually a rush, grows near the shore at the upper edge of the salt marsh. Rushes, similar to sedges and grasses,

Round-leaved sundew, Petit Manan NWR

have a flower structure that more closely resembles that of lilies. Sea lavender produces hundreds of minute flowers at the tips of wiry stalks in summer. The short, succulent stems of glasswort are edible. Less conspicuous are tiny green blossoms of coast blight, found in soils inundated by the highest tides.

■ ANIMAL LIFE

Birds The rugged refuge islands constitute vitally important nesting sites for seabirds. Petit Manan Island, two and one-half miles south of the point, is one of the most important sites for colonial nesting seabirds in the Gulf of Maine. Nash Island, seven miles south of the point, has nesting common eider, ducks, and gulls. Franklin Island hosts a dense common eider colony, while ospreys and black-crowned night herons nest in the trees there.

Treeless Seal Island, some 60 miles southwest of Petit Manan Point, was once home to the largest puffin colony in the gulf. The bird population was decimated from uncontrolled hunting and egg collecting; a model reintroduction project is under way (see Sidebar, p. 63).

After breeding on inland freshwater lakes, common loons come to saltwater to feed on the abundant fish. Other fish eaters include the double-crested cormorant, often seen standing on rocks with its wings stretched out in order to dry them. Black guillemots, medium-sized members of the auk family, are black with a bold white wing patch. In fall they molt, becoming mostly white. Common eider ducks (their down is legendary as an insulator both for the ducks and human-made products) feed on shellfish offshore, and small flocks begin assembling in late summer. Common terns and Arctic terns dive for fish in the chilly waters. Among the most attractive gulls are the 13-inch ternlike Bonaparte's and the somewhat bigger laughing gull, both of which wear black hoods during the breeding season. Bonaparte's show a good white slash near the wingtips.

In late summer, migrant shorebirds probe the flats for nutritious tidbits. Look for the banded semipalmated plover; the spotted sandpiper, which bobs incessantly; the long-legged greater yellowlegs; and the big willet. Away from the shore in wet places, look for telltale holes that plump woodcocks make as they probe for earthworms in the mud with long bills that have flexible tips.

Cormorant

Falcons follow the shoreline during migration, seeking sustenance from the thousands of shorebirds that also pass this way. In October, look for merlin and the larger peregrine falcon, reputed to be the swiftest bird in the world. The peregrine was hard hit by a combination of pesticides and human occupation and nearly became extinct in the eastern United States; numbers are being restored through restocking. Snowy owls often visit the area during winter when their Arctic food supply of lemmings and other rodents becomes scarce.

Ospreys are again fairly common breeders along the coast after being decimated by DDT contamination before the early 1970s. Two pairs nested near Birch Point in the late 1990s. In early August the loud, insistent, whistled begging calls of the one or two young can be clearly heard. Our national bird, the bald eagle, which was recently removed from the endangered species list (a true success story), feeds on dead fish—something the osprey never does—as well as the live ones it catches. Bald eagles begin nesting in March.

In summer, coniferous woodlands host 4-inch-long hyperactive golden-crowned kinglets searching for insects among the spruce boughs. Here, too, are warblers—beautiful bay-breasted, nuthatchlike black-and-white,

Atlantic puffins and sea spray, Petit Manan NWR

yellow-rumped, attractive black-throated green, and lovely Canada—a denizen of boggy habitats. On the forest floor, the russet-tailed hermit thrush delivers one of the most haunting and evocative songs of any on the continent. The beloved black-capped chickadee, the state bird of Maine, nests. Another species of chickadee, the boreal, is less common and much more retiring. Listen for its more nasal *chick-che-day-day* song.

The common raven weighs four times as much as a crow, being fully the size of a red-tailed hawk. Its deep, guttural croaks epitomize the north woods; notice its wedge-shaped tail and watch it ride air currents.

Reptiles and amphibians Eastern garter snake, that widespread and abundant species, is the refuge's most common reptile. You may see one of these snakes, which control their body temperature by behavioral means, basking in a sunny clearing. They test the air with their tongues, seeking the scent of frog, insect, or other edible creature.

Wood frogs rely on ephemeral vernal pools to lay their eggs in early spring. Common on the forest floor, they are difficult to see because of their camouflage. Almost the identical shade of light brown as dead red maple leaves, they lie in wait for insects. Vernal pools are also vital to several species of large burrowing "mole salamanders," including spotted and Jefferson.

Mammals White-tailed deer are the refuge's most commonly seen large herbivores. They munch herbs and shrubs in brushy fields near roadways, their reddish summer coats much brighter than the somber grayish-brown of fall and winter. Deer give birth to two or more spotted fawns in June. During winter, herds congregate in cedar swamps. Moose are also sometimes seen.

Evidence of porcupines is everywhere; examine jack pine and balsam fir trunks and branches to see where these spiny rodents have gnawed away the bark. They want the nutritious inner bark, or cambium. Among the most common rodents is the endearing red squirrel. With sharp incisors they attack spruce cones to harvest the nutritious seeds. Red squirrels also consume a fair amount of animal matter, including birds' eggs and nestlings.

PUFFINS Treeless Seal Island, 21 miles southeast of Rockland and some 60 miles southwest of Petit Manan Point, has boulder fields and ledges where Atlantic puffin, razorbill, and black guillemot lay their eggs. Terns prefer grassy spots, and eiders choose nest sites in the raspberry thickets. The unusual Leach's storm-petrel, a dainty 8-inch-long blackish seabird, nests in burrows it digs in the soft peat and glacial till soils. The abundant offshore fish population attracts the seabirds as well as namesake gray and harbor seals.

The island was once home to the largest puffin colony in the gulf. Uncontrolled hunting and egg collecting eliminated this engaging seabird from the island by 1887. Between World War II and 1952, the island was the site of military bombing and shelling. It is now the site of a model reintroduction project, sponsored jointly by the U.S. Fish & Wildlife Service, Canadian Wildlife Service, and National Audubon Society, aimed at restoring the Atlantic puffin and Arctic tern colonies.

Between 1984 and 1989, the society's Project Puffin, under the direction of Dr. Stephen W. Kress, introduced 950 puffin chicks from Newfoundland to the 65-acre island. Puffin chicks were hand-reared in artificial burrows. Part of the strategy involved using wooden decoys of the 10-inch-tall seabirds (complete with colorful beaks), mirrors, and sound recordings of their courtship calls to lure adult puffins to the island and keep them there. Amazingly, it worked. In 1992, 105 years after their departure as a breeder here, nesting Atlantic puffins once again called Seal Island home. The methodology, in fact, has been so successful that it is being used to reestablish nesting colonial seabirds elsewhere around the globe.

Some nesting gulls are being removed to prevent predation; decoys and sound recordings are used by biologists to attract Arctic terns back to the site, much as they were used to attract puffins.

Less than two and one-half inches long, diminutive masked shrews are frenetic, seeking out insects, worms, and virtually all things edible. Relying primarily on smell, they require nourishment nearly around the clock, sleeping only in fits. Owls include shrews in their diets, but foxes tend to forgo eating them, probably because of their musty odor.

Raccoons are widespread omnivores that feed opportunistically. During August nights, along with black bears, they gorge on the sweet blueberries that attract humans by day. Among the true predators, stealthy bobcats pounce on rodents and snowshoe hares that molt to white in order to blend into the winter landscape.

In offshore waters, harbor seals poke their snouts above the surface. They reside here year-round, giving birth to their pups on the islands. The much larger and less common gray seals prefer the more remote islands. A big male "horsehead" may weigh 800 pounds.

Fishes An abundance of fish-eating birds is testimony to waters rich in fishes. Saltwater species include the so-called groundfishes such as hake, cod, and flatfishes, which rely on the seabed for sustenance. These groups are some of the most commercially important species in the northwest Atlantic.

Invertebrates In sunlit meadows and along woodland edges, from late spring to fall, colorful butterflies live out their usually brief lives as adults, visiting flowers to sip sweet nectar and in the process performing important pollination services.

On foggy mornings, you can't help but notice the silken webs spun by spiders, each thread a dew-kissed strand of pearls hanging from the vegetation. Along the shore blackish "wolf" spiders, which don't build webs, dart among the rocks.

Exoskeletons of mollusks, crustaceans, and other saltwater creatures litter the shore. Look for blue mussels eaten by starfish and eider ducks among others, the soft-shell clams favored by humans, the small conical turrets of Atlantic oyster drills, and the round "tests" of green sea urchins. The white calcium carbonate homes of northern rock barnacles encrust boulders of the intertidal zone, and periwinkles rasp the alga off rocks with their file-like tongues. Check the small tidepools for scuds, sometimes called side swimmers. These inch-long crustaceans are related to the beach fleas found farther south along the coast.

You might see and hear a lobster boat making its rounds, checking baited cages marked by colorful floats to indicate their positions and owners.

ACTIVITIES

■ **CAMPING:** Camping is not permitted; public campgrounds are at Lamoine State Park in Lamoine Beach and Acadia National Park; a private campground is in Steuben.

■ **WILDLIFE OBSERVATION:** Each of the habitats of Petit Manan Point—fields, coniferous woodland, boggy wetland, and rocky shore—is accessible from two trails, Birch Point Trail and John Hollingsworth Memorial Trail. Take Birch Point Trail to its end to see nesting ospreys in April. Deer emerge from woodlands in summer at dusk to browse in fields. To visit some of the summer seabird colonies by boat, sign up for a guided trip. Migrant shorebirds comb the tidal flats in autumn, and rafts of eider form offshore. Winter's white blanket provides a fresh canvas for tracking mammals.

■ **PHOTOGRAPHY:** You won't want to get too close to a nesting osprey, so use a long telephoto lens to capture its beauty; a macro lens is best for photographing glistening spiderwebs. Weather conditions can go from foggy to bright sun in a matter of hours, so be prepared for changes in light intensity.

■ **HIKES AND WALKS:** The well-marked trails on Petit Manan Point lead through fragrant elfin forests of spruce, fir, and maple to gorgeous shores. The shorter John Hollingsworth Memorial Trail is the more strenuous of the two. The one-mile round-trip (out and back) begins at the small parking area at the trailhead. Birch Point Trail (the trailhead is on the same side of the road as the parking area) is three miles total; it leads gradually downhill and northward to lovely Birch Point, surrounded by Dyer Bay. It has two short side trails near its north end. The easterly one goes to Lobster Point, for great views. Maps are available at the trailhead. In winter, explore Petit Manan on snowshoes and cross-country skis. Anyone wishing to visit the islands should contact the refuge office first.

■ **PUBLICATIONS:** Two leaflets, "Petit Manan National Wildlife Refuge" and a refuge bird checklist, are available at the refuge office.

HUNTING AND FISHING Fishing is not permitted. The policy on deer and small-game hunting was being reviewed in 1999; it was anticipated that hunting would be permitted in some parts of the refuge, including some islands. Hunters are advised to contact the refuge office.

Sunkhaze Meadows NWR
Old Town, Maine

Peat bog, Sunkhaze Meadows NWR

Sunkhaze Meadows is an ecological gem. Its pristine peat marsh is the second-largest peat wetlands community in Maine. In some areas, the rich, pungent peat deposits are up to 18 feet thick. Unusual and rare species, including sundews, pitcher plants, and orchids, thrive here, taking root in a boggy terrain that is, literally, afloat.

Bogs are a finite resource, and have been since the last ice sheet melted away. Legend has it that bogs are shadowy places where evil vapors are emitted, home to the bad old bogey man. But bogs are in fact the habitat for some of the most fascinating plants on earth. Low oxygen levels, high acid levels, and low nitrogen have forced bog plants to adopt intriguing strategies for survival, including insectivorous habits. Because the high acid content and low oxygen levels retard decay, dead plant material tends to build up rather than decompose—the polar opposite of a tropical rain forest. As sphagnum moss and other plant material accumulate over decades and centuries, floating peat mats form gradually from the edge toward the center. In this floating ecosystem, even shrubs and small trees have been known to take root—and it is this habitat that is defined as a bog.

HISTORY

In the 1980s, interest from the peat-mining industry raised public awareness of the bog. Commercial plans fell through, and The Nature Conservancy purchased the area. The U.S. Fish & Wildlife Service acquired the property in 1988. The 10,000-acre property is currently visited by approximately 1,500 people each year, but the refuge plans to incorporate visitor facilities in future development.

The name Sunkhaze is from the Native American Abenaki phrase *wetchi-sam-kassek,* meaning "concealing outlet" and refers to the difficulty of finding the confluence of Sunkhaze Stream and the Penobscot River.

GETTING THERE

From Bangor, take I-95 north to Exit 51. Follow Rte. 2A (Stillwater Ave., then Center St.) east to Old Town, cross the Penobscot River to Rte. 2 in Milford; turn right after the light (County Rd.). Follow County Rd. 4.2 mi. to the refuge boundary.

■ **SEASON:** Refuge open year-round. No restroom or picnic facilities.

■ **HOURS:** Daily, dawn to dusk. Office (located at 1033 S. Main St., Old Town) open Mon.–Fri. 7:30 a.m.–4 p.m.

■ **FEES:** Free access.

■ **ADDRESS:** Sunkhaze Meadows NWR, 1033 S. Main Street, Old Town, ME 04468.

■ **TELEPHONE, FAX, AND E-MAIL:** Refuge Headquarters: 207/827-6138, ext. 10; fax: 207/827-6099; e-mail: R5RW_SHMNWR@fws.gov

WHAT TO SEE

Sunkhaze Stream and its six tributaries create a mosaic of wetland communities —wet meadow, shrub thicket, cedar swamp, extensive red and silver maple floodplain forest, open freshwater stream habitat, shrub heaths, and cedar and spruce bogs—best appreciated from a canoe. Peat deposits have been forming since the retreat of the last ice sheet 10,000 years ago. Deposits form where acidic conditions greatly retard decay, causing a buildup of dead sphagnum moss, sedges, and other bog plants. The refuge has several raised bogs or domes, separated from each other by extensive areas of streamside meadows.

The wetlands at midday are often bright and sunny, but in the mornings Sunkhaze Meadows can be shrouded in fog. Foremost among wetland shrubs is speckled alder, a birch relative that reaches 12 feet in height; moose and deer browse its twigs in winter. Male American woodcock spend their days in alder swamps and their spring evenings performing dazzling courtship displays at dusk for an audience of females.

Seven species dominate the boreal and northern hardwood forests of the refuge. Conifers include white spruce, balsam fir (long flat needles), white pine (five needles per bundle), and eastern hemlock (short, flat needles). The deciduous species are red maple, gray birch (the bark peels much less than that of white birch), and quaking aspen. Certain white pines, the state tree, are impressive, as are some hemlocks. Hemlock has a shallow root system and is subject to windthrow. When a hemlock falls, the uprooted tree creates the characteristic pit and mound topography. As the tree falls, a mound made up of soil and rocks once held within the rootball is left next to the pit where the roots were. Such woodlands are cool and damp, with little ground cover.

In mixed woodlands, the aptly named hobblebush spreads by suckers into foot-catching tangles. The large heart-shaped leaves turn maroon in late summer, and the clusters of white flowers (of two sizes) add light to the spring woodlands. While in the woodlands, listen for the deep hooting call of the barred owl. This large earless owl calls, *who cooks for you, who cooks for you all*. Porcupines are rodents renowned for their prickliness; their winter scat is oval and the consistency of sawdust—a result of their taste for the inner bark of coniferous trees.

Ferns grow abundantly in the damp partial shade; at least a dozen or so species are visible from the trails. You'll also spot different types of horsetails, a group of nonflowering plants that has changed little in 300 million years. The straight green, rough stems of this ancient group are common in damp soils.

Tussock sedge, which grows in clumps 2 to 3 feet in height, is a dominant plant in wooded swamps. Wetland communities show off many blooming plants in summer. Cardinal flower, one of our most beguiling native plants, entices hummingbirds. Two-lined salamanders seek daylight refuge under the flat stones of woodland brooks; flip over a few stones to see one scamper away—it will have a telltale yellow or green stripe bordered by a dark stripe running down its back.

Bullhead lily is a conspicuous wetland plant. Less noticeable are the small yellow pealike flowers of the bladderwort that poke out of beaver ponds. Bladderwort is one of the few plants that take needed nitrogen from tiny invertebrates that it captures underwater in its "bladders." The beaver handiwork is evident all over the refuge, and a canoe trip requires frequent carries over beaver dams. Large domed lodges provide shelter for a beaver family consisting of

SUNKHAZE MEADOWS HUNTING AND FISHING SEASONS

Hunting
(Seasons may vary)

	Jan	Feb	Mar	Apr	May	Jun	Jul	Aug	Sep	Oct	Nov	Dec
white-tailed deer (using following hunting methods)												
bows										■		
firearms											■	
muzzle loaders												■
moose									■			
black bear								■	■	■		
fox	■	■								■	■	■
bobcat	■									■	■	■
coyote	■	■							■	■	■	■
raccoon										■	■	■
cottontail rabbit	■	■	■							■	■	■
snowshoe hare	■	■	■							■	■	■
opossum										■	■	■
skunk										■	■	■
porcupine	■	■	■	■	■	■	■	■	■	■	■	■
woodchuck	■	■	■	■	■	■	■	■	■	■	■	■
red squirrel	■	■	■	■	■	■	■	■	■	■	■	■
gray squirrel										■	■	■
ruffed grouse										■	■	■
American crow		■	■				■	■	■			

Fishing
(Seasons may vary)

	Jan	Feb	Mar	Apr	May	Jun	Jul	Aug	Sep	Oct	Nov	Dec
brook trout				■	■	■	■	■	■			
chain pickerel				■	■	■	■	■	■			
smallmouth bass				■	■	■	■	■	■			
yellow perch				■	■	■	■	■	■			

The seasons for **American woodchuck, snipe, rails,** and **waterfowl** are set annually each September, just before the seasons start. Contact the refuge for the exact duration. Hunters at Sunkhaze must use nontoxic (nonlead) shot, and bear baiting is prohibited. **Moose** hunting requires a permit. Contact the refuge for permit information and any other information concerning current hunting and fishing seasons.

adults, two yearlings, and the young of the year, called kits. You may find the 6-inch-long tracks of a moose; a big bull can weigh more than 1,000 pounds. Many species of waterfowl use the refuge. In the wet meadows common snipe, a slimmer version of the russet woodcock, hunt for invertebrates.

The larvae of dragonflies and damselflies begin life as voracious predators on the bottoms of ponds. Adult females lay their eggs singly by touching the tips of their abdomens to the water's surface. Common species are the green darner and the black-winged damselfly. The male of the latter, a striking insect, has a metallic green body. It flies like a butterfly along refuge streams.

ACTIVITIES

The best way to see the refuge is by canoe. A trip down Sunkhaze Stream can begin from either of two access points, Ash Landing off Stud Mill Rd. and where County Rd. crosses Baker Brook at the refuge's southern end. Be prepared for frequent portages. If you are without a boat, the trail to Johnson Brook, about 1.5 miles out and back, makes a pleasant stroll. It is accessed from County Rd. and includes a loop.

In winter, you will need cross-country skis or snowshoes to get around. Use extreme caution when crossing any stream; it may not be completely frozen. A brochure is available from the headquarters office. Before setting out, check with refuge staff regarding the condition of trails indicated on the refuge map. Walking along the dusty perimeter roads is not recommended; heavy logging-truck traffic makes walking potentially dangerous.

Silvio O. Conte NWR
Turners Falls, Massachusetts

Connecticut River winding through southern New England

Conte is a pioneering refuge, a work in progress. For openers, it's massive and sprawling, encompassing 400 residential communities across four states, from the Canadian border to Long Island Sound. Second, Conte, as home to some 2 million people, represents more heavily developed lands than those traditionally slated for federal protection. The ground-breaking mandate of Conte is to engage the community of people who live in the Connecticut River watershed—11,000 square miles, the largest watershed in the region—in partnering with the refuge to protect the area's precious natural resources. It is for this precise reason that Conte was included in this book. While there is no refuge to see in the traditional sense, Conte represents the refuge system's continued challenge to provide a "web of life" for the survival of native wildlife, wildlife habitats, and precious ecosystems. Forging decision-making partnerships with the watershed's citizens—and involving them in the implementation of action plans—is the refuge's unique challenge in the years ahead. In addition, Conte is one of a handful of U.S. Fish & Wildlife refuges with a major focus on protecting and managing local fisheries habitats.

HISTORY

In 1991, President George Bush signed the act creating this four-state refuge, which was named in memory of the late Massachusetts congressman who dreamed of protecting the river for posterity. The law charged the U.S. Fish & Wildlife Service with studying the entire 7.2-million acre Connecticut River watershed (from Fourth Lake, high up in northern New Hampshire, to Old Saybrook, Connecticut, on the Long Island Sound) and creating a refuge. Refuge lands encompass a 3.8-acre island in Massachusetts, 278 acres in Putney, Vermont, and 18 acres in Westfield, Massachusetts. A likely addition of 26,000 acres in northeastern Vermont is pending.

It is the mandate of the Conte Refuge to work in partnerships with existing organizations to protect land, provide environmental education, and encourage and support appropriate wildlife habitat management on public and private lands. The refuge's 15-year goal is to restore 3,300 acres of wetlands, 900 acres of uplands, and 2,545 acres of streamside habitat.

GETTING THERE

To reach the refuge office in Turners Falls, take I-91 to Rte. 2 and follow it east to Gill. At the second traffic light (Avenue A/Main St.), turn right and cross the Turners Falls-Gill Memorial Bridge. The office and Great Falls Discovery Center are located in the second building on the right (until late 2000).

■ **SEASON:** Refuge office open year-round.

■ **HOURS:** Refuge office hours are weekdays, 8 a.m.–4:30 p.m.

■ **FEES:** Free access.

■ **ADDRESS:** Silvio O. Conte National Fish and Wildlife Refuge, at the Great Falls Discovery Center, 38 Ave. A, Turners Falls, MA 01376 (The Discovery Center was scheduled to open in 2000.)

■ **TELEPHONE, FAX, AND E-MAIL:** 413/863-0209; fax: 413/863-3070; The hearing impaired may call: 800/493-2370; e-mail: SOCNWR R5RW @mail.fws.gov; website: http://www.fws.gov/r5soc

WHAT TO SEE

There is as yet no refuge to see in the traditional sense. The refuge has very little real estate at present. But within the watershed, numerous projects are under way. Some are aimed at habitat restoration, others at environmental education, and still others at surveying and monitoring plant and animal populations. Preserving habitat within the watershed is essential to preserving viable populations of the more than 300 rare species (as well as an abundance of other species) living within the watershed. Species include freshwater mussels, tiger beetles, wood warblers, Atlantic salmon, and bald eagles. Many of these preservation projects are coordinated by partnering agencies and are carried out by volunteers.

A study to determine which migratory bird species use the Connecticut River as a migration corridor and exactly what habitat they require was conducted largely by 100 volunteers during three successive springs in 1996–1998. Each group selected a portion of the watershed to study as part of this "Migratory Bird Stopover Habitat Study." During the study's first year alone, 133 species were tallied. The larger focus of the study was an attempt to shed light on the causes for the decline of birds that winter in the New World tropics and breed in North America. The ultimate result could be the protection of vital refueling points for such neotropical migrants.

Other projects include grassland bird management in central Massachusetts, the monitoring of northern harriers in New Hampshire, development of a strategy for controlling invasive plants, river-herring restoration, and a juvenile salmon population estimate. This approach is ecological in the true sense in that it examines and responds to the interrelationships of all living things within the vast ecological unit of the Connecticut River watershed. The focus then is on the ecosystem rather than on one or more large glamorous species.

ACTIVITIES

You can visit a rare habitat occupied by many unusual species of plants at the Mollie Beattie Bog, 76 acres of black-spruce bog and surrounding buffer land in northeastern Vermont's Nulhegan Basin. A short boardwalk, which opened in 1997, leads to a platform overlooking the bog in the small town of Lewis.

Learn what a watershed is and how it functions by viewing the watershed exhibits at the Montshire Museum in Norwich, Vermont (802/649-2200).

Until 1999, when the eagles moved their nest to a new location about 100 yards distant, visitors could witness a pair of nesting bald eagles at Barton Cove in Gill on the Connecticut River in western Massachusetts. The huge nest was visible from the public boat launch off Rte. 2, in Gill. For two years, the eagles were television stars of sorts on a local cable television channel. Links to updated snapshots of the birds continue to appear on the refuge's web site. The birds who were present at the visible site from 1989, usually began nesting activities in February, with egg-laying during mid-March.

Watch Atlantic salmon and other anadromous fish (saltwater fish that return to their freshwater birth streams to spawn) moving up the Turners Falls Fish Ladder in May and June. A viewing window gives visitors a rare underwater perspective on this phenomenon, and a television camera sends images to the local access station as well as the Internet.

The Great Falls Discovery Center, scheduled to open in 2000, is a partnership of environmental organizations with the Conte Refuge. Visitors will be able to enjoy watershed maps, models, and habitat exhibits as well as interpretive programs and opportunities to observe local wildlife nearby. Brochures and newsletters about the local and watershed attractions and programs will be available.

Great Meadows NWR
Carlisle, Concord, and Sudbury, Massachusetts

Cattail marsh, Concord Unit, Great Meadows NWR

The overwhelming impression here is one of wetlands—a watery landscape of shrub swamps, cattail marshes, ponds, brooks, and bottomland forest, all throbbing with the vibrancy of life. Easy accessibility to a rich diversity of wildlife, along with the refuge's proximity to metropolitan Boston, makes Great Meadows one of the region's most-visited national wildlife refuges.

Every season holds magic at Great Meadows. In spring, red-winged blackbirds flaunt their gaudy epaulets as they hold forth from cattails. Fuzzy ducklings trailing their mothers swell summer waterfowl populations. The haunting sounds of migrant geese fill the deep-blue skies of autumn. River otters frolic and slide across the frozen snow-covered impoundments held in winter's grip.

HISTORY

A prominent attorney, sportsman, and member of a longtime Concord family, Samuel Hoar, purchased a part of the meadows in 1928. He constructed earthen dikes to impound the marshlands, making them even more suitable for waterfowl. In 1944 he donated 250 acres (Concord Unit) to the U.S. Fish & Wildlife Service. During the 1960s the service began buying additional lands. Today the refuge encompasses 3,400 acres with an additional 600 acres approved for acquisition.

Native peoples utilized the area seasonally for agriculture, hunting, and fishing; artifacts found on the property date back 7,500 years. They built fish weirs in the Sudbury River to trap fish and lived on what is now called Weir Hill. European settlers, who harvested floodplain hay, called the area Great River Meadows. Construction of a mill dam early in the 19th century caused water to rise and extend into the marshes, making the meadows too wet for farming. Today, more than 250,000 people visit the refuge each year.

Great Meadows also administers other refuge units (some of which are covered separately in this volume)—Oxbow, Monomoy, Nantucket, Mashpee, No Mans Island, Massasoit, and Assabet River in Massachusetts.

GETTING THERE

To reach the Weir Hill Unit, also referred to as the Sudbury Unit (refuge headquarters/Visitor Center): from Exit 26 off I-95/ 128, follow Rte. 20 west to Wayland. Turn right (north) at light onto Rte. 126/27 for .1 mi., then bear left and follow Rte. 27 north for 1.7 mi. Turn right onto Water Row Rd.; follow it 1.2 mi. to its end. Turn right onto Lincoln Rd. and drive for .5 mi. Turn left onto Weir Hill Rd. and follow signs.

To reach Concord Unit (Dike Trail Impoundments), from Exit 30 off I-95/Rte. 128, follow Rte. 2A west into Concord. Turn right onto Main St. (Rte. 62) and drive northeast toward Bedford for 1.3 mi.. Turn left onto Monsen Rd. and follow it .3 mi. to refuge entrance on left. Watch for the wooden stockade fence framing the entrance road.

■ **SEASON:** The refuge is open year-round.

■ **HOURS:** The refuge is open 30 minutes before sunrise to 30 minutes after sunset. Headquarters/Visitor Center open weekdays 8 a.m–4 p.m. The Visitor Center is often open 11 a.m.–5 p.m. May–Oct. weekends when staffing permits; closed weekends and holidays during winter.

■ **FEES:** Free access.

■ **ADDRESS:** Great Meadows National Wildlife Refuge, Weir Hill Road, Sudbury, MA 01776.

■ **TELEPHONE, FAX, AND E-MAIL:** 978/443-4661; fax: 978/443-2898; e-mail: R5RW GMNWR@fws.gov

TOURING GREAT MEADOWS

■ **BY AUTOMOBILE:** Automobiles limited to parking areas.

■ **BY FOOT:** Walking trails, in three main locations, total 3.2 miles in length; all are open to cross-country skiing.

■ **BY BICYCLE:** Bicycles are not permitted on refuge trails. Riding between units is possible; roads in the area experience fairly heavy auto traffic. Visitors may ride on an old railway bed not owned by the refuge.

■ **BY CANOE, KAYAK, OR BOAT:** Most refuge property is accessible only by boat. You may launch at Bedford Boat Launch (off Rte. 225, at the bridge over the Concord River), Monument Rd. bridge in Concord (at the Sherman Bridge, on Sherman Bridge Road in Sudbury), and on the Sudbury River at the Rte. 20 bridge in Wayland. A concrete canoe landing (not a launch site) is about 600 feet downstream from the Visitor Center at Weir Hill. Boating is not permitted on refuge pools in Concord. Boaters are asked to remove water chestnut plants from their boats and trailers so as not to transport the species to new sites.

Boats and canoes may be rented at South Bridge Boathouse (Rte. 62 in Concord). Note that rivers flood their banks in late March and April.

WHAT TO SEE

■ **LANDSCAPE AND CLIMATE** Only 12,000 years ago, retreating ice sheets left indelible marks on the land. Weir Hill is a deposit of glacial debris; its sandy soils are now clothed in oaks, pines, and pink lady's slippers. A chunk of glacial ice melted to form a kettlehole 200 feet in diameter between the hilltop trail and the adjacent wetland.

Fewer than 30 miles from the Atlantic Ocean, these swamps and woodlands

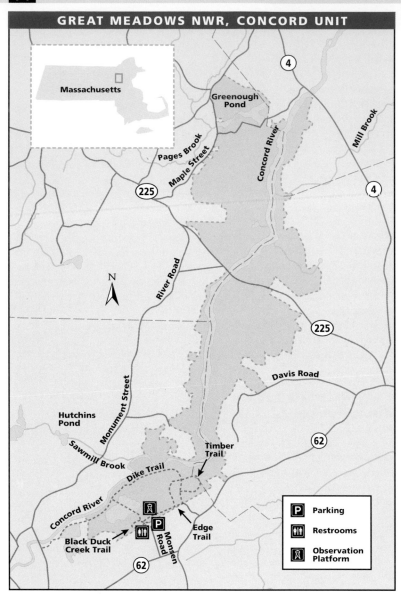

GREAT MEADOWS NWR, CONCORD UNIT

flourish in a climate modified by the sea. Summers are warm and can be humid, while winters are cold and moderately snowy.

■ PLANT LIFE

Marsh The dominant grass in refuge marshes—cattail—is one not often thought of as a grass. Both narrow- and broad-leaved cattails grow here, providing food, shelter, and nest sites for birds and mammals. The dry oak woods of Wood Duck Hollow Trail border an extensive cattail marsh, and the two impoundments are lined by thick stands.

Sedges are wetland plants related to grasses that have triangular stems. The most common is woolly sedge (or wool grass), whose fuzzy brown flower stalks reach five feet in height. Purple loosestrife, an invasive exotic, spreads by its roots and crowds out native vegetation. Beetles imported from Europe may aid in controlling its spread.

Red maple swamp A wooded swamp borders the Sudbury River in the Sudbury Unit. The crushed foliage of the sweetgale emits a spicy aroma. Small white "pompoms" cover the buttonbush in August. The sweet pepperbush does well in both swamps and sandy soils. These species, along with the speckled alder, silky dogwood, and the fragrant white-flowered swamp azalea, form a thick growth where soils are saturated for part of the year. The most numerous large trees, along with the maples, are black willows and eastern cottonwoods; in spring, the last launches millions of fluffy seeds on the wind.

Skunk cabbage is the earliest flower to bloom, while snow still blankets the ground. This odd plant produces its own heat (to 70 degrees F). The chestnut-colored tent-shaped spathe, which is easy to recognize, encloses the true flowers. By summer the leaves are 2 feet long and exude a pungent, musky odor.

Pine-oak woodland The Sudbury Unit (Weir Hill) is clothed in white pine and red oak. Other trees of the sandy uplands include white oak, pignut hickory, black cherry, and gray birch; the latter two colonize forest openings. Spicy, green-barked sassafras thrives as a small tree in these sunlit woods; its roots can be boiled to produce a pleasing tea. Lowbush and highbush blueberries are common.

Canada mayflowers carpet wide areas below white pines with delicate white flowers and shiny, heart-shaped leaves. The spotted wintergreen shows off variegated leaves, and wild geraniums open delicate pink blossoms.

Moist woods at the beginning of Weir Hill Trail host a thick growth of alder buckthorn, which has shiny, conspicuously veined leaves. Another shrub signifying wet soils is arrowwood, with arrow-straight branches. In rich woods near the kettlehole you will find black birch; its broken twigs smell and taste of oil of wintergreen. Sprouts of the American chestnut are mere remnants of the tree that once dominated the woodlands. The 1930s blight all but eliminated chestnut from the scene. Common witch hazel, known chiefly for its medicinal properties, puts out welcome, albeit straggly, yellow blossoms in autumn after leaves fall. The lovely dark-green foliage of the eastern hemlock adds a welcome contrast to the scene; it occupies the sloping kettlehole walls.

The higher, drier woods surrounding the marshland hold hop hornbeam, a small tree with flaky bark. Black locust, a fast-growing, thorny legume, develops three-inch-long seedpods. Below the trees, in the dry, nutrient-poor soils, are the pink blossoms of sheep laurel (said to be poisonous to sheep). The deep-green wavy-edged leaves of the sweet fern, 2 feet tall, exude a pleasant aroma.

WATER CHESTNUTS A most troublesome alien exotic, the water chestnut once choked 80 percent of the two waterfowl impoundments, substantially reducing their wildlife value. Introduced into this country in the late 1800s, water chestnut appeared in the Sudbury River in the 1950s; it was found in refuge impoundments in 1978. Floating plants are rooted in the bottom muck and form an almost impenetrable surface mat that crowds out native vegetation. Herbicides used to combat water chestnut also killed native vegetation. Mechanical harvesting has markedly reduced this invasive, although harvesting does not destroy the seeds. Periodic draining may do so.

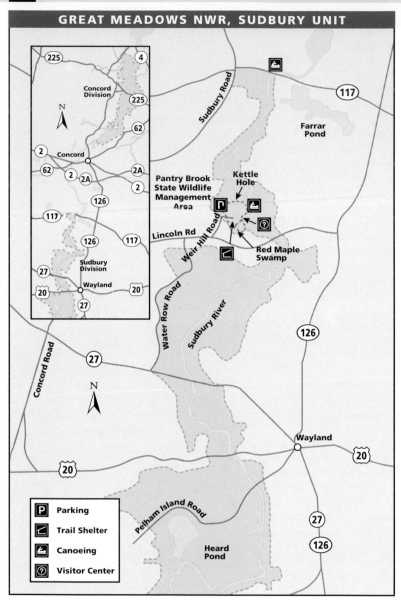

GREAT MEADOWS NWR, SUDBURY UNIT

Legend:
- **P** Parking
- **◪** Trail Shelter
- **⛵** Canoeing
- **ⓘ** Visitor Center

Mapleleaf viburnum has three-lobed leaves (velvety below) reminiscent of its namesake. A 10-foot shrub whose nuts are relished by wildlife grows at the edge of the forest; American hazelnut fruits are enclosed in beaked husks.

Ponds and impoundments Midsummer constitutes the peak flowering period for many aquatic plants. Pickerelweed produces spikes of bluish-purple florets, while arrowhead exhibits fewer white-petaled ones. American lotus sports impressive pale yellow blossoms and great bowl-shaped leaves.

Less showy in the shallow water is bur reed, whose flower heads become spiky orbs. The bladderwort consumes minute creatures by sucking them into tiny submerged bladders when they brush against the plant; its yellow pealike flowers protrude from the water. Duckweed forms a floating green mat on still waters; the minute flowers are rarely seen. Yellow iris is an attractive foreigner at the edge of the pond.

■ ANIMAL LIFE

Birds The refuge checklist contains more than 220 species, 85 of which have nested. The variety of plovers and sandpipers during fall migrations can be quite dramatic. Scan September mudflats for stilt sandpipers, chunky dunlin, and occasional white-rumped sandpipers.

Although the marsh is too shallow for diving ducks, the dabbling American black ducks, blue-winged teals, and wood ducks breed here. The 1938 hurricane destroyed many dead trees that had provided nesting cavities for wood ducks, and the population plummeted. Wooden nest boxes were substituted, and this elegant acorn eater is once again common. Because wood-duck hens often "dump" their eggs in the nests of other females, you may see a hen trailed by 20 or more young. American wigeon and gadwall migrate in large numbers during the fall.

You will likely see black-crowned night herons, crow-sized green herons, stately great blues, and an occasional egret stalking frogs and fish. From the dike, watch for reclusive marsh birds (sora and Virginia

Wood duck

rails), especially just before dusk in August, when they are on the move.

In summer, marsh wrens weave nests in cattails that fringe the impoundments; males fashion several "dummy" nests, perhaps in an effort to frustrate predators. Listen for their mechanical songs in June. Swamp sparrows also breed in marshes, as well as the northern waterthrush, a striped ground-nesting warbler that bobs continually. Alder and willow flycatchers, small, closely related birds once thought to be the same species, sing distinctive songs in the shrubby wetland habitats where they breed.

Summer woodlands provide habitat for the cavity-nesting great crested flycatcher, yellow-billed cuckoo (declining over much of its range), russet wood thrush, brilliant scarlet tanager, rose-breasted grosbeak, and Baltimore oriole; pendulous oriole nests hang high in the trees.

Nocturnal raptors range in size from the 8-inch eastern screech owl to the "earless" 18-inch barred owl to the imposing 2-foot-tall great horned owl, capable of dispatching skunks.

Mammals Half a dozen bat species, our only flying mammals, spend daylight hours in hollow trees, buildings, or, in the case of the red bat, in foliage. At dusk they give chase, employing sophisticated sonar to capture insects. Muskrats construct lodges of cattail stalks and mud in the relative safety of the marsh, where they dine on a variety of foods, including cattail tubers.

Red and gray foxes help keep rodents in check, pouncing on their prey with rigid forelegs. The gray fox is a surprisingly small animal with retractable catlike claws that allow it to climb trees.

Reptiles and amphibians Female painted turtles dig nests with their hind

Marsh wren

feet in well-drained earth, lay half a dozen eggs, and cover them with soil. After three months of solar incubation, the leathery eggs hatch and the tiny young make their way to water; look for evidence of nest predation by raccoons in sandy soil around the pond adjacent to the red maple swamp. Snapping turtles, up to 2 feet in length, are also common, but are seen basking far less often; the danger they pose has been exaggerated.

The eastern garter is the snake that you are most likely to meet. The black racer, one of the largest of the seven resident species, can attain a length of 6 feet. Snakes often take advantage of solar-heated road pavement in the evening and many thus lose their lives. The note of a plucked banjo string alerts one to the presence of a green frog. On spring evenings listen for the deafening sleigh-bell chorus of inch-long spring peepers. Wood frogs quack like ducks in their woodland pools. Vernal pools, those ephemeral water bodies, are also obligatory breeding sites for the 6-inch spotted salamander, with its unmistakable lemon-yellow polka dots.

Fishes In June brightly colored pumpkinseed sunfish defend nests in the shallows of the Sudbury River at the canoe landing and along the Concord Unit dike. The female fans her fins to make a shallow depression, then lays her eggs for the male to fertilize. Also look for brown bullheads from the dike in June, and for tadpole-like juveniles in the shallows.

Big nonnative carp find their way into the impoundments when the Concord River overflows its banks each spring.

Invertebrates Damselflies and dragonflies spend most of their lives as aquatic larvae. Highly carnivorous as nymphs and adults, they fly rapidly and hover on gauzy wings. At rest, the smaller damselflies fold their wings over their backs. Green darner, our largest dragonfly, the easily identified whitetail dragonfly; short-stalked damselfly; and Doubleday's bluet are common near water.

Oak forests are defoliated periodically by gypsy moths, first imported to Massachusetts from Europe in 1869. The hairy caterpillars, feeding at night, may completely strip a tree. The visual impact is stunning. Trees eventually regrow leaves, a "second spring" of sorts. Repeated infestations over a period of years can kill trees. Look for fuzzy tan-colored egg masses, containing some 400 eggs, on trees or artificial structures.

ACTIVITIES

■ **SWIMMING AND CAMPING:** Not permitted. The nearest public campground is in Harold Parker State Forest in North Reading (20 miles northeast of Concord).

■ **WILDLIFE OBSERVATION:** Wildlife can be approached from a canoe. But if you're on foot, the dikes that bisect and traverse the edges of impoundments make the Concord Unit especially rewarding; observe nesting marsh wrens, rails, American bitterns, and other elusive marsh denizens there. In late summer and early fall, after water levels are lowered to expose mudflats rich with invertebrates, shorebird watching may be spectacular. Later in the fall, migrant ducks and geese, often in large numbers, make stopover appearances. An observation tower at the parking area affords views of the marsh.

Woodland birding is outstanding in spring from the Weir Hill Trail. Bird feeders are maintained at the Visitor Center.

■ **PHOTOGRAPHY:** Morning light is best for taking photographs. Views from the observation tower are panoramic. Early spring wildflowers in the Weir Hill area woodlands make pleasing subjects.

■ **HIKES AND WALKS:** Of the three trails, Dike Trail is by far the most walked. The 1.7-mile loop leads you over the dike separating the impoundments and then (right) around the Lower Pool's perimeter back to the parking area over an old railroad bed. You can also turn left at the end of the dike, follow along Upper Pool to a dead end, and then retrace your steps to the dike. These paths are broad and level; during wet springs, they may be flooded.

In the Weir Hill area walk the slightly more than one-mile loop trail through pine-oak woodlands and along the edge of Red Maple Swamp; view the scenic Sudbury River at the canoe landing. The trail, via switchbacks, climbs and descends Weir Hill, a vertical rise of 80 feet. Maps are available at the Visitor Center.

Wood Duck Hollow Trail, near the southern end of the Sudbury Unit, is a .5-mile loop that begins at a small roadside parking area and proceeds through oak forest; a side path (the second right) ends at a cattail marsh.

HUNTING AND FISHING Hunting is not permitted in the refuge; it is permitted in the Pantry Brook State Wildlife Management Area bordering the Sudbury Unit. Fishing is permitted on the Concord and Sudbury rivers but not in refuge pools.

■ **SEASONAL EVENTS:** Numerous public programs are conducted throughout the year for children and adults at both units. Events include the Nature Arts and Crafts Show (mid-May), Wildlife Week (April), and Rivers Night (June).

■ **PUBLICATIONS:** Two brochures, "Great Meadows National Wildlife Refuge" and "Birds of Great Meadows National Wildlife Refuge," are free at the Visitor Center. Receive the quarterly newsletter, "The Meadows Messenger," by writing the refuge office.

Monomoy NWR
Morris Island, Chatham, Massachusetts

Dunes and salt marsh, Monomoy NWR

Serene and untamed, Monomoy is a landscape shaped by the sea. Broad tidal flats, dotted with shorebirds, give way to amber dunes swept by persistent onshore winds. Monomoy retains the attributes of unblemished coastal terrain largely spared the human hand. Though only 10 miles off the elbow of the vacation mecca of Cape Cod, this barrier island is one of the most enchanting locations on the New England coast. During vernal and autumnal migrations, thousands of shorebirds make this slim finger of sand their home.

HISTORY

Monomoy Island got its name from the Monomoyick tribe, Native Americans who occupied the Chatham area hundreds of years ago. The refuge was established in 1944. In 1970, Congress designated 2,450 acres (94 percent of the refuge) as a federal wilderness area. Only two tracts on South Island and the refuge's mainland portion were excluded. Today, the refuge, administered by Great Meadows NWR, encompasses 2,750 acres and is visited by 45,000 people annually.

Native Americans led the first European ships around Monomoy Point past the shoals to safety. Samuel de Champlain, forced ashore in 1606 by a broken rudder, named the spot Cape Batturier, while other Frenchmen called it Cape Malabar—"cape of evil bars," in reference to its treacherous shoals and sandbars. The Pilgrims, on glimpsing the dangerous Pollock Rip Shoal, headed the *Mayflower* back to what is now Provincetown.

The island's first fishing village was established near Inward Point, on what is now the northern tip of South Monomoy, in 1711. Another fishing village once thrived on South Monomoy; clues of former habitation such as scraps of rusted metal, wood, and stone are still visible amid the shifting sands of the Powder Hole area.

Stately Monomoy Point Lighthouse was constructed on South Monomoy in

1836, decommissioned in 1923, and renovated in 1988. Bearing witness to the shifting nature of a barrier island, it now sits, stranded, one-half mile from the ocean.

GETTING THERE

To reach Morris Island headquarters, take Rte. 6 east to Exit 11 (Rte. 137). Follow Rte. 137 for about 3 mi. to Rte. 28. Follow Rte. 28 east for about 3.5 mi. to the rotary in the center of Chatham. Turn south onto Stage Harbor Rd. for 1 mi. and then left onto Bridge St. Turn sharply right (south) after .8 mi. onto Morris Island Rd. Follow it across causeway and onto the island. Continue past "residents only" sign and take first left onto Wikis Way.

- **SEASON:** Refuge open year-round.
- **HOURS:** Refuge: Dawn to dusk. Headquarters: 8 a.m.–4:30 p.m.
- **FEES:** Free access; tour/boat fees separate.
- **ADDRESS:** Monomoy NWR, Wikis Way, Morris Island, Chatham, MA 02633.
- **TELEPHONE, FAX, AND E-MAIL:** 508/945-0594; fax: 508/945-9559; e-mail: R5RW_MNWR@fws.gov

TOURING MONOMOY

- **BY AUTOMOBILE:** Monomoy is a roadless area.
- **BY FOOT:** Walking is the only way to get around, but there are no formal trails on North and South Monomoy. Access to portions of both is restricted in spring and summer to protect nesting birds. Do not walk on dunes that have vegetation. Tour groups of six or more must obtain a permit; call 508/945-0594. A .75-mile-long trail on Morris Island leads to the beach.
- **BY BICYCLE:** Bicycles are of no use on the islands.
- **BY CANOE, KAYAK, OR BOAT:** North and South Monomoy islands are accessible only by boat. Canoes and sea kayaks are not recommended for travel to South Monomoy, given the currents; boats can generally land only on the Sound (west) side of the islands. Avoid waters off Monomoy Point altogether because of sandbars, riptides, and a strong chop. The best way to see the islands is via guided tours operated by the Cape Cod Museum of Natural History and the Massachusetts Audubon Society. Ferry service alone is available from Monomoy Island Ferry, Captain Keith Lincoln (508-945-5450). Trips to the north and south islands take 10 and 30 minutes, respectively. South Island is especially difficult to reach in bad weather.

WHAT TO SEE

- **LANDSCAPE AND CLIMATE** The islands, extensive dunes and tidal flats, all constantly shifting, were formed of sand deposited by ocean currents off Cape Cod's elbow. At one time the entire refuge was connected to the mainland, but a storm separated most of it from the mainland in 1958. In 1978 another storm broke the island one-fourth of the way south, forming North and South islands. Small- and large-scale changes continue; a chain of small islands is now forming between the two islands. North Island is 1.8 miles long and .5 mile wide at its widest point; South Island is 5.5 miles long and 1 mile wide at its widest point.

The sun's rays, reflected by sand and surf, create a blindingly bright light; it can be hot in low spots protected from the wind. Summer mornings may be very foggy. In early spring and late fall, the weather is often unpredictable and harsh. Getting to the islands in any season depends largely on the vagaries of the sea and the weather.

■ PLANT LIFE

Dunes American beach grass, the dominant refuge plant, stabilizes the dunes. Large areas are also covered by gray-green clumps of false heather, a characteristic dunes species that puts forth tiny yellow flowers in early summer. Among the most primitive land plants are pale green reindeer lichen, which grows on sterile sand. In interdunal areas, yellow-blossomed sickle-leaved golden asters bloom in late summer. Dry sandy areas also host pearly everlasting, which flowers earlier. The tiniest flowers are those of mudwort (white), which grows in "grassy" mats on the sand.

Backdunes No trees grow on North or South Monomoy; woody vegetation consists primarily of the fragrant bayberry (wax myrtle), which yields large quantities of hard wax-covered berries devoured by tree swallows and yellow-rumped warblers. Poison ivy, whose berries also represent valuable wildlife food, sometimes attains shrub size here. In late summer its leaves turn shades of yellow, orange, and crimson. Both shrubs also provide important cover for wildlife and nest sites for birds, and help stabilize the backdunes.

Tidal flats and salt marsh Blackish algal mats stranded on the mudflats by the receding tide are the most primitive plants found here and indicate a submerging coastline. (Sea levels are gradually rising.) But the most important grasses are the Spartinas: tall saltwater cordgrass and the shorter, often prostrate, salt-meadow cordgrass. Black grass, actually a sedge, grows along the margin of the Powder Hole. Sea lavender may bloom in profusion in late summer on the tidal flats; the flowers of seaside gerardia are also lavender. The salty edible stems of slender glasswort, a short, succulent, segmented plant also known as pickleweed, turn translucent red in late summer.

Freshwater ponds The tall chairmaker's rush thrives along the shores of South Monomoy's freshwater ponds, together with various sedges and common reed, also known by its scientific name, *Phragmites*. A fairly large stand waves 12-foot-high feathery seed heads at Big Station Pond on South Island. Familiar cattails are found here as well. In late summer along the shores of freshwater ponds, robust rose mallow bushes bloom, unfurling large and photogenic pink cups. Here too are the small but attractive scarlet pimpernel, common skullcap (blue flowers), salt-marsh fleabane, spearmint with pinkish blossoms and a square stem, and horehound, with its small white flowers clustered close to the stem.

Haircap moss grows in moist spots, and bog (marsh) club moss in a small boglike area on South Island. Cranberry seems out of place in the impoverished, acidic soil of the "bog." Its small but lovely pink flowers emerge in June. Marsh fern, identified by thick leaflets with rolled-under edges, grows near pond edges.

Pine-oak woodland The 40-acre Morris Island portion of the refuge is partly wooded with pitch pine, scrub oak, and red oak.

■ ANIMAL LIFE

Birds Monomoy is a key Western Hemisphere staging area for more than 30 species of migrant shorebirds that pause here after their brief Arctic breeding seasons. Indeed, in late summer and fall this is a premier shorebird viewing location on the Atlantic seaboard. Rarities that have turned up include black-tailed and bar-tailed godwits and Eurasian curlew.

Some 60 species nest in or near the refuge, the most notable being piping plover and least tern. Large red-beaked and yellow-legged American oystercatchers nest on Inward Point at the north end of South Monomoy. Other shorebird breeders include willet and spotted sandpiper. The aptly named black skimmer

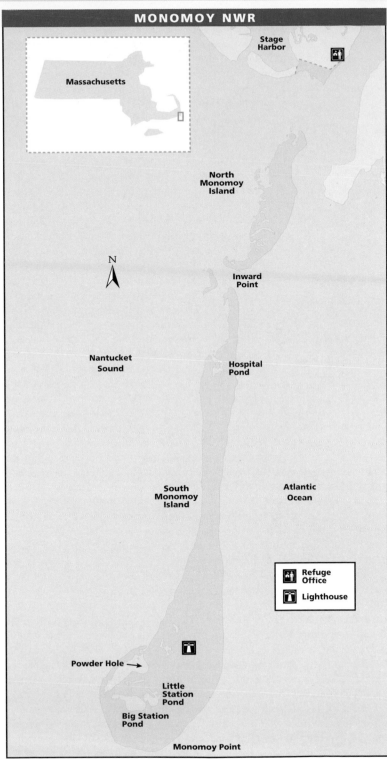

MONOMOY NWR

Massachusetts

Stage
Harbor

North
Monomoy
Island

N

Inward
Point

Nantucket
Sound

Hospital
Pond

South
Monomoy
Island

Atlantic
Ocean

Refuge
Office

Lighthouse

Powder Hole →

Little
Station
Pond

Big Station
Pond

Monomoy Point

nests as far north as Monomoy, and in summer you may see these birds slice the water with their outsized beaks.

Black-crowned night-herons, snowy egrets, and the elusive sora and Virginia rails breed in the South Monomoy wetlands. The freshwater ponds also provide nesting habitat for black duck and, in fewer numbers, gadwall, blue-winged teal, northern pintail, and northern shoveler. Ubiquitous herring and great black-backed gulls are common nesters, to the detriment of breeding terns. These large gulls were not originally southern New England nesters, but the proliferation of

open landfills in the late 20th century made possible tremendous population growth. Interdunal areas were once littered with the bodies of dead gulls that did not survive their first year. On North Monomoy, at the state's only breeding colony of laughing gulls, these birds sport black heads during the breeding season and cut loose with a maniacal laugh.

The relatively few breeding land birds include savannah sparrow in the dunes and common yellowthroat (males have a black mask) in freshwater wetlands. Sharp-tailed sparrows breed in the saltwater marsh vegetation on North Monomoy.

In the fall, southbound ducks and geese rest and feed in freshwater and brackish ponds. The most common include ring-necked duck

Herring gull

and green-winged teal (the smallest of our ducks); ponds are also feeding grounds for glossy ibis, great egrets, great blue herons, and the occasional tricolored and little blue herons. Endangered roseate terns (the adults have a delicate pink wash on the breast) rest here prior to their fall migration to the West Indies and South America. Nearly the entire population of this bird breeds off southern New England. Black terns, inland nesters, are regular, albeit uncommon, migrants in late summer; look for them around freshwater ponds.

Large concentrations of common eider ducks (of eiderdown fame), white-winged scoter, and red-breasted merganser winter just offshore, arriving in the fall and returning to their Canadian breeding grounds in the spring. An estimated 108,555 common eider wintered in 1991, feeding on the abundant blue mussels and other shellfish. Scaup, common goldeneye, old-squaw, and canvasback also arrive in October and November.

Mammals Monomoy's most fascinating mammals, the harbor and gray seals, fish just offshore and haul out on refuge beaches in winter. Gray seals are called horseheads because of their ample muzzles; males may reach 800 pounds. In recent years they have bred here. Harbor seals have a more delicate pointed snout and are much smaller; large males weigh perhaps 250 pounds. These curious and engaging aquatic mammals poke their heads out of the water to reconnoiter as your boat passes by.

A herd of some 20 white-tailed deer live on South Monomoy, and your chance of seeing them is good; watch for their tracks in the mud at the edge of a pond.

Abundant meadow voles live in the grassy dunes of both islands and run for the cover of bayberry thickets when startled. Although there are no mammalian predators, voles are pursued by northern harriers and short-eared owls. Muskrats, about the size of a small cat, burrow into the soft soil at the edges of freshwater ponds. They eat both plant and animal material; here they relish fresh-water clams.

Reptiles and amphibians Reptiles are scarce on North and South Monomoy; the ubiquitous common garter, primarily brown, is the only resident snake; they feast on toads, fish, and insects. Offshore, large sea turtles—green, hawksbill, loggerhead, and ridley—occur seasonally.

The only amphibian on the islands is the 2-inch-long sand-colored Fowler's toad, which digs into the sand with its hind feet to protect itself from snakes and to escape the heat of the day. This toad was named after a 19th-century amateur naturalist from Massachusetts. Large dark splotches on its back contain many small "warts," or poison glands. In late summer you will find many of these engaging little creatures hopping about. Once common on other islands off the coast, they were eradicated by aerial DDT spraying for mosquitoes in the '40s, '50s, and '60s.

The small, partly wooded Morris Island portion of the refuge has spotted and red-backed salamanders and green frogs in addition to Fowler's toads. Spotted salamanders, black with bright yellow polka dots, breed in the spring in woodland pools.

Fishes Largemouth bass, stocked in freshwater ponds years ago by refuge staff, still thrive today. But introduction of this nonnative predator caused problems for some smaller species. Mackerel sometimes turn up in the shallows of Powder Hole at low tide. Bluefish, striped bass, and other saltwater game fish lure anglers to the refuge. Nesting terns feed on the numerous sand lance—small, silvery eel-like fishes important in the diets of predatory fish, seabirds, and great whales. Little skates are often washed ashore, as are their black egg cases, known as "mermaid's purses."

Gray seals awaiting the return of high tide, Monomoy NWR

Invertebrates Beachcombers will find surf clams (at 7 inches across, the largest), soft-shelled clams (the "steamers" of restaurants), channeled whelks, northern moon snails, and blue mussels. Crabs include spider, mole, and lady crab, which has a speckled shell. You will find horseshoe crab shells (not a crab at all but in fact a member of the arachnid, or spider, family) of all sizes in tidal areas. Horseshoe crabs are called "living fossils" because they have survived on Earth for millions of years. Clam worms, which burrow into the soft mud of tidal flats, are sought out by shorebirds.

Late-summer butterflies include American painted lady, pearl crescent, and monarch. Dozens of the big orange and black monarchs fatten up on goldenrod nectar while migrating to Mexico. Predatory green darner dragonflies and smaller damselflies patrol the skies, especially near fresh water, while predaceous diving beetles hunt for prey in the ponds. Plant-eating sand-colored grasshoppers and field crickets are abundant in the dune vegetation.

Black-legged (deer) ticks are present; these tiny creatures can transmit Lyme disease to humans; wear pants and shirts with long sleeves if possible and check yourself carefully for ticks after you leave. Biting greenhead flies may be a nuisance in summer.

ACTIVITIES

■ **SWIMMING AND CAMPING:** Sunbathing, swimming, and wind surfing are popular. A sandy bathing beach is at the southwest end of South Monomoy near the Powder Hole. Camping is not permitted. The nearest campgrounds are at Brewster, Dennis Port, and Eastham. The Cape Cod Museum of Natural History (508-487-9410) accommodates 20 at the Monomoy lighthouse for special programs.

■ **WILDLIFE OBSERVATION:** Harbor and gray seals swim just offshore, especially between Nauset Beach and North Monomoy. The largest shorebird concentrations are found on North Monomoy's Godwit Bar within three hours of high tide in late July and early August; the variety actually increases from late August to early September. At high tide, when the birds are concentrated, the Powder Hole is the premier shorebird location on South Island. You may see nearly 20 species

Marbled godwits

HUNTING AND FISHING Off-shore **surf-fishing** is allowed throughout the refuge, and you can enjoy 24-hour fishing access on Morris Island. **Striped bass** and **bluefish** are the most common catches. **Clamming** for **soft-shelled clams** ("steamers") is also a possibility; you simply need to secure a town permit beforehand. One favored location is Powder Hole. For information on current license requirements, seasons, and bag limits, consult the refuge office. Hunting for off-shore **waterfowl**, specifically **ducks** and **geese**, is allowed only at the mean tide line and below. The seasons for waterfowl hunting are set annually each September, just before the start of the season. Check with the refuge for this year's schedule.

during a single visit. Portions of both islands are closed during the summer piping plover and least tern nesting seasons.

In late summer, warblers and other land birds rest on South Monomoy prior to their long overwater migrations to the tropics. Huge flocks of tree swallows fatten up on the nutritious bayberries. An average day in late summer will yield about 50 bird species; in all, 285 species have been recorded.

■ **PHOTOGRAPHY:** Opportunities abound for both scenic and wildlife photography. For shorebirds, the Powder Hole area of South Island is a good spot. Seals make fascinating subjects as they poke their heads out of the water or lie on the beaches. Remember that bright sun and sand reflect much light, so you may have to close your lens down a stop or two to counter it.

■ **HIKES AND WALKS:** A .75-mile trail traverses pitch pine-scrub oak forest, ocean beach, and salt marsh at refuge headquarters; steps are involved. At the south end of South Monomoy, you will walk several miles on packed and loose sand from the beach near the Powder Hole to Big and Little Station ponds and back. On North Monomoy, you will walk about 1.5 miles from the beach to Godwit Bar and back. Stay off the dunes. Guided tours are the best way to discover these islands.

■ **SEASONAL EVENTS:** Monomoy lighthouse (508/487-9410) is a base of operations for extended natural and cultural history tours.

■ **PUBLICATIONS:** Headquarters has a bird checklist.

Nantucket NWR
Nantucket, Massachusetts

Walking the beach, Nantucket NWR

This remote and isolated northern tip of Nantucket Island is an untamed spit of sand where the sea lords over the fragile earth. Here, at Great Point, the terrain is ever reshaped and refined by the coastal elements. In all seasons this island—the "gray lady" of legend—embodies both austere beauty and serenity. Birds in great number and variety rule the food chain on the refuge.

HISTORY

In the Algonquian language, Nanticut meant "faraway land." The island, a terminal moraine, or pile of earth and stones delivered to this spot by glacial activity, about 25 miles from Cape Cod, became a Quaker stronghold, then an international whaling center, in the early 19th century. Great Point Light, dating from 1784, was destroyed twice, then relocated to its present site within the refuge and restored in 1986. The 40-acre refuge, established in 1973 and now visited by more than 100,000 people each year, is administered by Great Meadows NWR.

GETTING THERE

Auto ferries depart from Cape Cod's Hyannis (508/540-2022; 2.5 hrs., summer); be sure to reserve space for your car well in advance. Commercial airlines fly from Hyannis, Martha's Vineyard, Boston, and Providence. Once on Nantucket, drive your own or rented four-wheel drive, oversand vehicle north from Wauwinet for 7 mi. A permit must be obtained from The Trustees of Reservations (TTOR), which controls access to the refuge.

■ **SEASON:** Refuge open year-round. Sections of the beach may be closed to vehicles, May–Aug. (piping plover and least tern nesting season).
■ **HOURS:** Open 24 hours
■ **FEES:** Free access.

■ **ADDRESS:** Nantucket NWR, c/o Great Meadows NWR, Weir Hill Road, Sudbury, MA 01776.

■ **TELEPHONE, FAX, AND E-MAIL:** Refuge Headquarters: 978/443-4661, 978/443-2898; TTOR Property Manager: 508/228-3359; e-mail: R5RW_GMNWR@fws.gov

WHAT TO SEE

■ **LANDSCAPE AND CLIMATE** Nantucket and other large southern New England islands are moraines built up before the glacier's retreat 12,000 years ago. Wide sandy beaches and windswept dunes, topped by American beach grass, seaside goldenrod, and showy saltspray rose, define Great Point, which is sometimes cut off from the rest of the island by powerful storms. Sand and water reflect sunlight to produce a desiccated place virtually without shade, while other days can be leaden and rainy.

■ **PLANT LIFE** The waxy berries of the bayberry provide high-octane fuel for tree swallows and yellow-rumped warblers. In early fall, poison ivy's red foliage contrasts with the sand; its berries are gobbled up by birds. Migrant monarch butterflies sip fat-rich goldenrod nectar in late August and September.

■ **ANIMAL LIFE** Fowler's toad, once common on Nantucket, was extirpated by aerial spraying of DDT for mosquitoes in the '40s, '50s, and '60s. Meadow voles, deer mice, and short-tailed shrews (a subspecies found nowhere else) are abundant, but tracks in the sand are usually all that you will see. All three provide sustenance for winged raptors. (Nantucket has no native mammalian predators.) Three tree-dwelling bats—hoary, silver-haired, and red—wing southward during migration in late summer. Carnivorous bluefish depart Nantucket in early fall. Watch for telltale oil slicks when they attack schools of small "baitfish" such as Atlantic silversides. Bluefish and striped bass are popular with anglers.

Least terns

Birds The refuge is a tiny but important resting and feeding area for shorebirds, seabirds, and migrant land birds. Gale winds force migrants to the island's sheltering vegetation. Birding is best from mid-September through mid-October. Great Point harbors nesting colonies of the threatened least and common terns. The endangered piping plover, so named because of its high-pitched plaintive call, also breeds in small numbers; three nesting pairs were reported in 1999.

During the winter, Nantucket is home to enormous concentrations of sea ducks—scoters, eiders, and old-squaws. An astounding 158,924 old-squaws, comely ducks with long pointed tails, were tallied during the 1992 Christmas bird count. Fish-eating common loons spend the winter in these waters, and you may glimpse the colorful male harlequin duck. Big white northern gannets dive for fish from 100 feet up.

A sizable population of hawks and owls call the island home year-round. The rodent-hunting northern harrier breeds here, as do fish-eating ospreys and red-tailed hawks. In fall, winter, and early spring, be alert for the endangered peregrine falcon, merlin (a smaller falcon), and sharp-shinned hawk. A few barn owls and short-eared owls occasionally nest on the island; snowy owls sometimes winter. The winter months are also the most opportune season to find the odd harbor or gray seal (grays breed as far south as Monomoy NWR, 10 miles north. See page 80). Whales and dolphins appear occasionally.

ACTIVITIES

TTOR's guided tours, May-Columbus Day, provide the best way to see the refuge. No formal trails exist, but it's an easy walk along the beach to Great Point, then on a four-wheel-drive track through dunes past the lighthouse (chemical toilet here) for a few hundred yards. It's a tough but scenic seven miles from Wauwinet (where the pavement ends) to the Point. Although bicycles are popular on the island, they are of no use in the refuge's soft beach sand.

The TTOR staff leads a three-hour guided natural history tour of the NWR, which includes a visit to the lighthouse (even to the top for a view). Tours take place from mid-May through mid-October and by group charter during the off-season. TTOR maintains the lighthouse structure by arrangement with the Coast Guard, while the USCG maintains the light itself. The NWR borders Coskata-Coatue Wildlife Refuge, which is protected by TTOR and a local conservation agency. This entire area has 20 miles of trails and protects 18 miles of ocean beach.

Oxbow NWR
Harvard, Shirley, and Ayer, Massachusetts

On the boardwalk, Shrub Swamp, Oxbow NWR

Water is Oxbow's defining factor. The slow, meandering Nashua River nurtures wetlands and rich floodplain forests. A plethora of aquatic creatures, from goggle-eyed dragonflies to rare Blanding's turtles, owe their existence to the refuge's life-giving water. In the formation of the refuge's namesake oxbow ponds—the offspring of a lazy river—the dynamics of the watery landscape continue to play out.

Agriculture, industry, and, more recently, commercial development have all taken their toll on the region's riverbanks and floodplain forests, among the country's most imperiled natural habitats. Today, the precious resources of these freshwater wetlands have been preserved for all to enjoy.

HISTORY

Established as a refuge in 1974 by transfer from the Department of Defense, Oxbow currently encompasses 1,547 acres. Oxbow is administered by Great Meadows NWR. Forty-three thousand people visited the refuge in a recent year.

GETTING THERE

From junction of the Mass. Turnpike (I-90) and I-495 (exit 11A), take I-495 north for 12 mi. to exit for Rte. 117. Follow Rte. 117 west for 3 mi. Turn right (north) on Rte. 110 and drive 3 mi. to Still River Depot Rd. on left. If you're coming from Harvard Center (the town, not the university), follow Rte. 110 south from the town for 1.8 mi. and turn west onto Still River Depot Rd. The refuge entrance and parking lot are across the railroad tracks and adjacent to the river.
■ **SEASON:** Refuge open year-round.
■ **HOURS:** Open 30 minutes before sunrise to 30 minutes after sunset.
■ **FEES:** Free access.
■ **ADDRESS:** Oxbow NWR, c/o Great Meadows NWR, Weir Hill Road, Sudbury, MA 01776.

■ **TELEPHONE, FAX, AND E-MAIL:** Refuge headquarters (Great Meadows NWR): 978/443-4661; fax: 978/443-2898; e-mail: R5RW_GMNWR@fws.gov

TOURING OXBOW

■ **BY AUTOMOBILE:** Motorized vehicles are not permitted beyond the parking area.

■ **BY FOOT:** Several miles of trails traverse the property. Because the refuge may have once been used as a bombing site by the Department of Defense, metal detritus is occasionally found. If you come across any unusual metal objects, report them but do not touch!

■ **BY BICYCLE:** Bicycling is not permitted on the refuge.

■ **BY CANOE, KAYAK, OR BOAT:** Boating on the Nashua River provides an enjoyable way to observe Oxbow's vegetation and wildlife. Put in at the parking area's step-ramp canoe launch. Because the current is usually tranquil, traveling upstream in summer is seldom a problem.

WHAT TO SEE

■ **LANDSCAPE AND CLIMATE** The refuge's namesake ponds were so described because of their resemblance to the wooden yokes used to restrain oxen. But oxbow ponds are not the refuge's only distinguishing feature. Shrub swamps, beaver flowages, bottomland forest of red maple, and the meandering Nashua River dominate the landscape. All that water can produce high relative humidity during the summer months. In contrast, the refuge's sandy pine oak woodlands can be sunny and dry. Born as a result of glacial activity, these dry, sandy stretches are vegetated with oak, pine, birch, and sweetfern. Some low, windswept dunes have no vegetation at all to hold sand grains in place.

> **OXBOW PONDS** Oxbow ponds were named for their resemblance to the old wooden yokes once used to restrain oxen. Oxbow ponds develop from an aging river's tendency to wander from its original straight course. As it does, it forms loops.Water must flow faster around the outside of a loop than along the bend's inner bank. The added momentum scours the outside bank. Over time this cutting causes the river to take a shortcut across the neck of the loop, creating an oxbow. The isolated crescent of former river channel then lies totally cut off from the ever dynamic main channel. Once exiled from the river, oxbow ponds begin the process of filling in.

■ **PLANT LIFE**
Freshwater wetlands Some oxbows are filled with buttonbush shrubs that display white 1-inch globular flower heads like so many pompoms. Tussock sedge forms mounds that so closely resemble stepping-stones that visitors might be tempted to use them to cross the swamp—but don't! Rank growth of reed canary grass fills wet meadows. The ribbonlike leaves of water celery float on the slow-moving river; damselflies use the leaves for landing pads. The surface of standing water supports a scum of tiny duckweed and minute watermeal, perhaps the smallest blooming plant (.5-1.5 millimeters) in the world.

The season's first flowering plant, skunk cabbage, produces its own heat, enabling it to melt through the snows of late February; its bruised leaves emit a

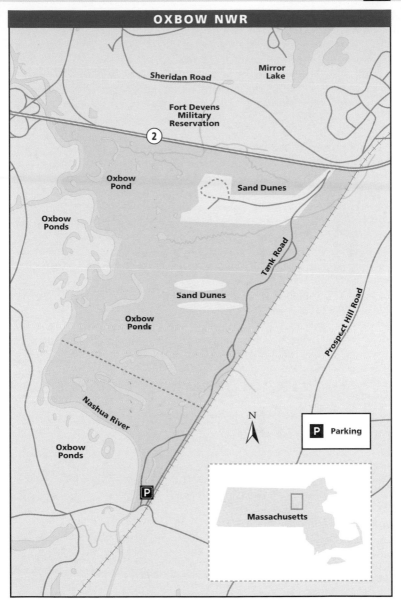

OXBOW NWR

Sheridan Road

Mirror Lake

Fort Devens Military Reservation

2

Oxbow Pond

Sand Dunes

Oxbow Ponds

Tank Road

Sand Dunes

Oxbow Ponds

Prospect Hill Road

Nashua River

N

P Parking

Oxbow Ponds

P

Massachusetts

fetid odor. In summer, blue flag iris and pickerelweed—an emergent with a spike of purple flowers—add color to the wetlands. In midsummer, look for yellow bullhead lily, purple swamp milkweed, and pink swamp rose.

Floodplain (riparian) forest The predominant tree of the periodically inundated bottomland forest is the adaptable red maple. Big, mottled American sycamore and silver maple (its deeply lobed leaves are silvery beneath) line the rivers' banks; their roots help stabilize the soil, and the hollow trunks provide dens for raccoons, flying squirrels, bats, and other creatures.

Transition forest Trees reminiscent of both northern and southern New England intermingle at Oxbow to form an intermediate, or transition, forest.

Black cherry (prized by furniture makers), elm, and big-tooth aspen, which attains large size here, are common. Growing in sandy soils, white pine is a pioneer that has become a major component of the bottomland woods in the floodplain; it is also expanding among the oaks.

Two other conifers, pitch pine, a tree of sandy coastal plains, and balsam fir, a species whose wonderful fragrance evokes thoughts of the cool, damp north woods, grow here. Hazelnut, which produces tasty nuts for wildlife, and alder buckthorn, which has shiny leaves with prominent veins, both dwell in the diminished sunlight below the taller trees.

Woodland spring flowers include false Solomon's seal, red baneberry, wild oats (with yellow drooping flowers), enchanter's nightshade, and common violet. You will find the eye-catching orchid pink lady's slipper in June in acidic, needle-covered ground. One of the most attractive midsummer flowers is Canada lily, whose large yellow bells hang by ones and twos in the damp woods.

Old fields Old fields regenerating to woodland contain small pioneering gray birch, white birch, and quaking, or trembling, aspen. Meadowsweet, a pink-flowering shrub, grows among them. Lowbush and highbush blueberries also thrive in sterile soils, producing sweet fruits in late summer. The fragrant but misnamed sweetfern borders woodlands.

■ ANIMAL LIFE

Birds Woodland breeding birds such as thrushes, vireos (including yellow-throated), and wood warblers are common. During spring migration, many additional species frequent the refuge. Connecticut warblers, rare consumers of insects, have turned up.

Belted kingfishers appear by streams; a rattling call identifies the blue-crested big-billed birds. Spotted sandpipers teeter along the shore; males incubate the

Old fields returning to woodland, Oxbow NWR

Eastern painted turtle

eggs. The great blue heron, a study in stealth, fishes in ponds and backwaters. The chunky American woodcock hides by day in alder swamps, probing for earthworms, and sings its long, twittering courtship flight song at dusk.

Wood ducks, among our most splendid waterfowl, nest in oversized nest boxes; they are fond of acorns. During migration, ospreys search the river for fish. The great horned owl, our largest owl, resides near the river, though seldom seen.

Reptiles and amphibians The 7-inch-long Blanding's turtle, listed by Massachusetts as a threatened species, is the refuge's most notable reptile inhabitant. Eastern painted and snapping turtles are also common.

Wetlands, many and varied, provide great habitat for frogs and toads. Commercial poachers have severely impacted leopard frog populations in some places. Wood frogs, like some salamanders, require woodland vernal pools for breeding. Gray tree frogs and spring peepers are less often noticed unless calling in spring.

Mammals Beaver dams and lodges are common sights. Aspen is their favorite food; watch for recently felled trees near the trails. Habitats created by these amazing rodents attract many other creatures, including muskrat, river otter, mink, waterfowl, amphibians, and aquatic insects.

By moonlight raccoons hunt for crayfish, frogs, and other life along the pond shores. In late summer, ripe fruits make up a large part of their diets; scat (droppings) are all that you will usually find. White-tailed deer roam the refuge.

At dusk, the skies fill with the acrobatic flight of some half-dozen bat species as they hunt insects in the warm night air, guided by sonar. In late summer some species migrate; others seek caves and abandoned mines in western New England.

Invertebrates Butterfly-watching is great in summer, especially along the tank road. An inventory of rare species has been conducted. Dragonflies and damselflies are also well represented. An iridescent green-bodied species, the ebony jewelwing, or black-winged damselfly, frequents running water; its fluttery flight and striking appearance call attention to it.

Speedy and highly predaceous tiger beetles hunt the sunny areas with sandy soils. Their larvae dig vertical burrows into the sand and wait for passing insects to come within reach of their powerful jaws. Along the river shore, long-legged spiders walk on water, entertaining humans as they skate on the surface film. These fishing spiders live up to their names by catching fish.

ACTIVITIES

■ **WILDLIFE OBSERVATION:** Whether you paddle a canoe or walk the trails, opportunities for spotting birds and butterflies abound. This is also a great place to see reptiles and amphibians. Breeding woodland birds make music from late May to early July, especially early in the day. Large numbers of waterfowl assemble in the wetlands during fall migration.

■ **HIKES AND WALKS:** A well-blazed trail turns left from the tank road, .35 mile from the parking lot, closely parallels the river for .75 mile, then turns right and rejoins the road. This straight attractive stretch (.7 mile) across shrub wetlands is an old stage road; turn right, back to the parking area (.6 mile).

Next, walk the tank road for about 1.3 miles north to Rte. 2. Then double back and swing westward, traversing low dunes; after about .6 mile, you must retrace your steps to the parking area.

Long sleeves and insect repellent protect against summer mosquitoes and deer flies; be alert for poison ivy; precautions against ticks should also be taken.

■ **PHOTOGRAPHY:** The scenic Nashua River lends itself to landscape photography from canoe or trail. Wildflowers such as pink lady's slipper, Canada lily, and swamp rose are tempting subjects, although you will need a telephoto lens for roses well out into the swamp. Butterflies are lovely, albeit challenging, subjects. From bright dune areas to shady bottomland forest, exposures will vary widely.

■ **CAMPING:** Camping is not permitted on refuge property. Public campgrounds are at Pearl Hill State Park in West Townsend and Willard Brook State Forest in Ashby and Townsend; 508/597-8802.

■ **PUBLICATIONS:** A leaflet, "Oxbow National Wildlife Refuge," is available from Great Meadows NWR.

OXBOW HUNTING SEASONS

Hunting (Seasons may vary)	Jan	Feb	Mar	Apr	May	Jun	Jul	Aug	Sep	Oct	Nov	Dec
ring-necked pheasant	░	░	░	░	░	░	░	░	░	■	■	░
common snipe		░	░	░	░	░	░	░	░	■	■	░
ruffed grouse		░	░	░	░	░	░	░	░	■	■	░
gray squirrel		░	░	░	░	░	░	░	░	■	■	■
cottontail rabbit	■	■	░	░	░	░	░	░	░	■	■	■

The hunting of upland game birds and small game is permitted in accordance with Massachusetts state hunting regulations and open hunting seasons. The hunting of waterfowl and white-tailed deer is not permitted. The **American woodcock** season is set each September, just before the season begins. Check with the refuge for the exact dates. Bow and arrow and shotguns are the only hunting methods permitted. All vehicles are restricted to the designated parking area accessible from Still River Depot Road. Unleashed dogs are permitted only while under the control of individuals actively engaged in hunting. The use or possession of alcoholic beverages while hunting is prohibited. For information on current license requirements, seasons and bag limits, consult the refuge office.

Parker River NWR
Newburyport, Massachusetts

Salt marsh and estuary, Parker River NWR

Golden beaches pounded by surf, flowing dunes sculptured by wind, expansive salt marshes teeming with life, and the tranquil waters of Plum Island Sound all combine to create the many moods of Parker River NWR. Sandwiched between the vast Atlantic to the east and a biologically rich estuary at the confluence of three rivers to the west, Plum Island's sandy spine is a grand legacy of the last ice age. Only 35 miles north of Boston, this refuge safeguards one of the Northeast's few remaining unspoiled barrier beach systems and its many living inhabitants.

HISTORY

Long before Europeans arrived in the New World, indigenous Massachuset people established spring fishing camps in the area. Shellfish middens, flint projectile points, and pottery shards found at several sites are the only remaining traces of their culture. Samuel de Champlain explored the coastline in 1605, and Captain John Smith mapped it in 1614. Smith provided the first written account of the island's plum thickets.

Farming played a major role in the area's economy for two centuries after European colonization with the harvesting of salt-marsh hay. During the era of market hunting in the mid-1800s, numerous hunting camps shot down countless thousands of birds for the dinner table.

The refuge was created in December 1941 by the merger of a 1,600-acre bird sanctuary, acquired by the Massachusetts Audubon Society in the mid-1930s, and 3,000 acres acquired by the federal government.

Parker River, at 4,662 acres, is one of New England's most popular refuges, with about 250,000 visitors each year.

GETTING THERE

From I-95 (Exit 57), travel east on Rte. 113 for about 3.5 mi. to Newbury. At the traffic light turn left onto Rolf's Ln.; follow Rolf's Ln. for .5 mi. to its end at the Plum Island Turnpike. Turn right and follow the Plum Island Turnpike over the bridge. At the first intersection, Sunset Dr., turn right and continue about .75 mi. to the entrance gate.

For refuge headquarters, north of the refuge proper, continue straight (east) past Sunset Dr. to Northern Blvd. and turn left (north). Follow Northern Blvd. for about 1.4 mi. to headquarters on the left.

■ **SEASON:** Refuge open year-round; April–Aug., beach closed.

■ **HOURS:** Refuge: Sunrise to sunset. During the warmer months the refuge sometimes fills to capacity and is subsequently closed for several hours.

■ **FEES:** $5/vehicle or $2/individual if entering on foot or by bicycle. Annual passes ($12) available.

■ **ADDRESS:** Parker River NWR, 261 Northern Blvd., Plum Island, Newburyport, MA 01950.

■ **TELEPHONE, FAX, AND E-MAIL:** 978/465-5753; fax: 978/465-2807; e-mail: R5RW_PRNWR@fws.gov

TOURING PARKER RIVER

■ **BY AUTOMOBILE:** The refuge road is paved as far as the Hellcat Wildlife Observation Area; for the lower three miles, the road is gravel that can be very dusty in dry summer. Parking is permitted only in designated lots. Four-wheel-drive vehicles, for fishing access only, may access the beach on two ORV trails when the beach is open (mid- to late August to October); permit required.

The western portion of the refuge, west of Plum Island Sound, is far less visited. Rte. 1A provides access to Parking lots 8 and 9 (Area C, Nelson's Island). Lot 9 is open to birders; check at the refuge headquarters to see if the area is open to hunting during waterfowl season.

■ **BY FOOT:** Enter at the gatehouse on Sunset Dr.; walk-in access to refuge from the beach is not permitted. You may walk the 6.5-mile partly paved refuge road, but traffic and dust may be problems. Three trails totaling 2.3 miles begin at parking adjacent to the refuge road areas (4, 6, Pines). Walk only on beach boardwalks or the shore and do not cut across dunes. The beach is closed from April to August to protect nesting piping plovers and least terns.

■ **BY BICYCLE:** Bicycling is best in early morning before traffic and dust intensify. Bicycles are not permitted on trails.

■ **BY CANOE, KAYAK, OR BOAT:** Watercraft provide access to Plum Island Sound, the Merrimack, Parker, and Ipswich rivers, and the tidal salt marsh, but landing or launching boats on refuge property is prohibited. You may come ashore on Sandy Point State Reservation at the southern end of Plum Island; consult tide tables and Reservation Headquarters (978-462-4481). You can kayak the Plum Island estuary from Ipswich to Newbury and the Merrimack River estuary.

WHAT TO SEE

■ **LANDSCAPE AND CLIMATE** Retreating glacial ice 12 millennia ago dropped mounds of rock, gravel, and sand to form hills called drumlins on five sites at the southern end of what would become Plum Island. Silt from the rivers and sand washed ashore by the sea created the barrier beach, which protects Plum Island Sound and the salt-marsh ecosystem from the full fury of Atlantic storms. Wind is ever-present on the island's windward flank. On the leeward face of the dunes, calmer air currents and sunlight intensified by buff-colored sand create a significantly warmer microclimate.

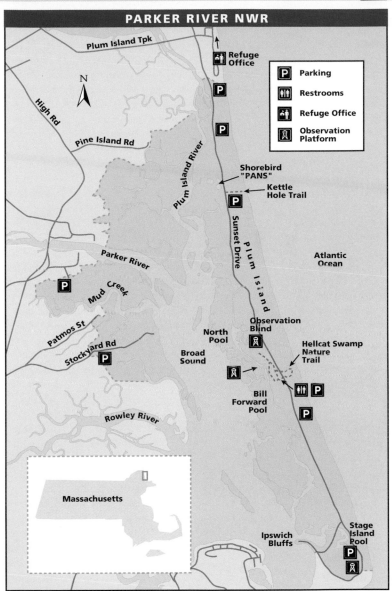

PARKER RIVER NWR

P	Parking
🚻	Restrooms
👫	Refuge Office
🔭	Observation Platform

Plum Island Tpk

N

High Rd

Pine Island Rd

Refuge Office

Plum Island River

Shorebird "PANS"

Kettle Hole Trail

Parker River

Mud Creek

Sunset Drive

Plum Island

Atlantic Ocean

Patmos St

Stockyard Rd

North Pool

Broad Sound

Observation Blind

Bill Forward Pool

Hellcat Swamp Nature Trail

Rowley River

Massachusetts

Ipswich Bluffs

Stage Island Pool

As in other coastal areas, spring is generally chilly. Onshore breezes provide a respite from summer heat and biting flies, while fall is often pleasantly mild because of the sea's ameliorating effects. Northeasterly gales and drifting snow can create Arctic-like winter conditions.

■ **PLANT LIFE** During the first 100 years after European colonization, settlers took advantage of the area's luxuriant plant growth to graze hogs, cattle, and horses. The indiscriminate grazing wrought considerable damage to the island's native vegetation until 1739, when uncontrolled grazing was declared illegal. The introduction of exotic plants was a further detriment. In the time since the refuge was created, nearly 60 years ago, a combination of fire controls, planting, and restrictions on foot and vehicle traffic has helped to stabilize many dunes by enabling native vegetation to reestablish itself.

Dunes Beach grass binds the fragile dunes with its extensive root system. The sand-colored, foot-long cylindrical seed heads of this attractive grass wave in the ocean breezes. One of the most emblematic of dune plants, silvery-green false heather flourishes as low-growing mats in these sterile soils. The yellow flowers open in June. Stay on the boardwalk and admire the blossoms from afar. At that time of year, the delicate and fragrant blossoms of wild rose are also evident. In late summer and early fall seaside goldenrod, another dune species, puts forth its large showy spike of tightly clustered yellow flowers; insects find them irresistible.

Plum Island took its name from native beach plums that grow profusely in the sand. This small tree's frothy-white May blossoms produce delicious inch-long fruit in September. Wild cherry also colonizes and stabilizes the dunes. Mammals and birds eagerly seek out its small black fruits. Bayberry, or wax myrtle, is another keystone species of sandy soils in southern New England. It thrives in thicketlike profusion here, producing large quantities of fragrant wax-coated "berries." Birds such as yellow-rumped warblers consume this fat-rich winter food. Colonists boiled down the fruits for candle wax. Even the leaves exude a delightful aroma.

Salt marsh Between the dunes and the mainland, rich salt marshes thrive, nourished by the constant movement of fresh water into the estuary as well as the lunar ebb and flow of the tides. In the black muck of the brackish (fresh and salt-water mix) salt marsh, spartina, or cordgrass, the dominant plant, reaches 6 feet in height along tidal creeks. It provides food and cover for many creatures.

Freshwater marsh From late June to August, purple loosestrife, a magenta-colored exotic invasive from Eurasia, blooms in the freshwater marshes. Although attractive, it benefits virtually no native wildlife as it relentlessly crowds out cattails and other important natives.

Greater yellowlegs

Woodland The small heart-shaped leaves of the quaking aspen, one of the refuge's primary trees, produce a soothing rustle. Another broadleaf species is red maple, whose leaves turn a blazing scarlet in autumn along Interpretive Trail. The most noticeable trees are probably the pitch pines in two distinct groves. Identified by short, stiff needles that often grow directly from the trunk, these pines are modest in stature by inland standards.

■ ANIMAL LIFE

Birds One of the finest birding locales anywhere along the Atlantic flyway, Parker River NWR serves as vital resting and feeding ground for migrants. As a cul-de-sac, it acts as a land-bird "migrant trap" where, especially in the fall, there are excellent views of a multitude of avian species (305 observed). Because rarities and out-of-range species show up regularly, you might find almost anything.

Highlights: thousands of migrant ducks and geese in early spring; notable migrant songbird fallouts in May; a purple martin nesting colony; southbound shorebirds (more than 30 species) from July through September; herons and egrets; and a splendid fall waterfowl and land-bird migration. Lightning-fast peregrine falcons follow the coastline, feasting on the unwary among the shorebird flocks.

In winter, Arctic raptors feed on a meadow vole bounty. Statuesque snowy owls resemble mounds of snow in the salt marshes. Northern harriers course low over fields and wetlands, listening for scurrying voles. Rough-legged hawks hover on broad wings, scanning the ground for reckless mice. Offshore, eider and scoter ducks float on the waves, occasionally diving for shellfish meals.

Mammals Look for white-tailed deer, the largest mammals on the island, early and late in the day. You might spot a red fox hunting for

THREATENED PIPING PLOVERS

Every spring the federally threatened piping plover, a sand-colored six-inch-long shorebird, returns to the protected sandy beaches of Parker River refuge to nest. The piping plover takes its name from its high-pitched call. Along with the least tern, a state-listed species of "special concern," the plover battles mammalian and bird predators, as well as careless humans and their vehicles, which destroy the plover's nests and young. (In 1995, 21 pairs of plovers produced 44 chicks; in 1997, 16 pairs produced 20 chicks. Prior to closing the beach, the refuge averaged 2-3 pairs with little or no young produced. Since closures were instituted, the refuge averages 12-13 pairs producing 20 chicks) Because the mere presence of humans may keep plover and tern mothers away from their chicks for dangerously long periods of time, refuge beaches are closed during the plover's nesting season.

rodents in the fields or dunes. At dawn and dusk during June and July, fox kits sometimes frolic along the refuge road. Striped skunks and raccoons, which will eat almost anything, are common but seldom seen. Red squirrels chatter in the pitch pines. Woodchucks emerge from winter dormancy in late March or early April. Cottontail rabbits are among the most frequently seen refuge mammals year-round. The beaver, a luxuriantly furred semiaquatic rodent, dwells in North and Bill Forward pools.

Harbor seals and an occasional heftier gray seal congregate in winter off the rocky ocean beaches at the southern end of the island. Periodically they bask on a glacial rock exposed by a falling tide.

Reptiles and amphibians Although snakes are seldom seen, the eastern garter is common; its diet includes insects, amphibians, and small mammals. Another medium-length brown snake, a mouser, is the eastern milk snake—identified by a light Y or V at the back of the head and a checkerboard underside.

Two species of turtle live at Parker River. The one you are most likely to see, in freshwater pools and wetlands at the float from April, is the eastern painted turtle. Averaging 6 inches in length, it has attractive reddish coloration on the lower shell. Less common is the snapping turtle—the largest growing to a length of 2 feet.

Countless tiny spring peepers cling to cattails and sing their sleighbell-like

Red fox in snow

song en masse during the first mild, wet nights of early spring. Later, breeding choruses of the American toad produce a loud, vibrating trill in freshwater marshes and pools. Northern leopard frogs, with brown blotches, prowl the moist grassy swales in search of insects. Green frogs, intermediate in size between the two, and with parallel "pleats" down their backs, emit humorous plucked banjo-string gulps. The unusual and threatened spadefoot toad occurs here too. The most numerous salamander, the red-backed, can be seen in the deciduous woodlands of the refuge.

Fishes Tidal saltwater and freshwater flowing into Plum Island Sound from three rivers and many smaller creeks intermingle to produce a rich broth teeming with microorganisms, the base of the food pyramid. Many commercial fish species spawn and spend the early portions of their life cycles in these salt marshes. A fish census of the sound during 1993-94 found 33 species. Among the most numerous of small estuary fishes are mummichog and silversides; other species include northern pipefish (as long and thin as its name implies), flounder, and four species of sticklebacks. Stickleback males are renowned for the spirited defense of their nests. American eels, 3 or4 feet in length, search for food in the tidal channels, often becoming meals themselves for cormorants and great blue herons.

There are also species that, as adults, adapted to life in ocean waters—striped bass, bluefish, and dogfish shark. The striped bass, a popular game fish, migrates to the area from southern waters in mid-May and departs each October.

Invertebrates One of North America's best-known insects, the monarch butterfly, makes a 2,000-mile journey to the Transvolcanic Mountain Range in central Mexico each autumn. En route, it refuels on fat-rich nectar sources such as the seaside goldenrod found here. Mosquitoes and biting greenhead flies make their presence known, especially from mid-July through August. Ticks, some capable of transmitting Lyme disease, are often present on vegetation. Staying on marked trails and wearing long-sleeved shirts and long pants will minimize your exposure to them.

Tidal marshes teem with crabs, mollusks, and other aquatic invertebrates. Sand shrimp are among the most abundant Broad Sound creatures and serve as dinner for many predators. Tiny colonial fiddler crabs, waving out-sized claws, dwell in burrows excavated in muddy tidal marshes, while larger green crabs live in the estuary, and lady crabs and spider crabs reside in salty ocean waters.

ACTIVITIES

■ **CAMPING:** Camping is not permitted; try nearby Salisbury Beach State Reservation, Rte. 1A, Salisbury, MA (978-462-4481).

■ **SWIMMING:** Sunbathing and swimming are popular at Parker River NWR when the beach is open. Swimming is at your own risk; currents and undertows may be strong. Swimming is also permitted at adjacent Sandy Point State Reservation.

HUNTING AND FISHING Surf **Fishing** is allowed beginning in July in areas not closed because of nesting birds. Both night fishing and 4-wheel-drive vehicle access require a permit.

Waterfowl hunting seasons for **geese, ducks, American coot**, and **sea ducks** are set in August and usually last from October to February. A controlled **deer** hunt is conducted annually on the island section of the refuge, at which time all other public access is prohibited.

Clamming is popular, and clammers go in search of "steamers" in designated refuge areas. Unfortunately, Plum Island Sound is often closed to shellfishing because of bacterial pollution. Stormwater runoff seems to be the major source of this contamination. Faulty septic systems, agricultural fertilizers, and illegal discharge of wastes from boats also contribute to the problem. A network of volunteers monitors the situation.

Check with refuge headquarters for refuge clamming access regulations. However rains usually close the clamming flats. To get the latest status of the flats, call 970/356-6671.

■ **WILDLIFE OBSERVATION:** You can observe wildlife at parking areas along the road—sometimes without leaving your car, as at the Salt Pans. Better yet, park and walk the loop trails. The first major shorebird viewing area, at shallow tidal pools known as the Salt Pans, is just over one mile south of the entrance. At high tide this is the single best place from which to see numerous species of plovers and sandpipers. A spotting scope is useful for studying the plumage subtleties of shorebirds and other species here and for scanning the ocean waves on the opposite side of the dunes for loons, grebes, and diving sea ducks.

Wildlife observation towers at Hellcat and Stage Island Pool permit a bird's-eye, if somewhat distant, view of geese, ducks, herons, egrets, and other wildlife. An observation blind is situated at one end of Hellcat Interpretive Trail. From late spring to midsummer, observe the purple martin colony from the deck adjacent to the restroom building at Parking Lot 1, and from the Hellcat parking area and other points along the road.

When bad weather forces migrating land birds (warblers, orioles, vireos, flycatchers, etc.) to take refuge, the island's trees and bushes can be festooned with small feathered bodies searching for the insect food that will sustain them for the next leg of their long flight.

September is when the monarch

butterfly migration spectacle is at its peak. On a good day you may glimpse hundreds of these butterflies winging southward over the dunes.

■ **PHOTOGRAPHY:** The Salt Pans are an excellent place from which to photograph shorebirds, herons, egrets, and ducks at moderately close range, especially during morning hours when light is best. Using your vehicle as a blind, you can sometimes approach birds and mammals quite closely. Morning is best at the observation blind on Hellcat Interpretive Trail.

Salt marshes, dunes, and the red maples along Hellcat Trail all take on lovely autumn hues during late October and early November, and miles of nearly pristine ocean beach provide opportunities for photography. The panoramic scenes from the top of the Dunes Trail boardwalk are splendid.

■ **HIKES AND WALKS:** Sturdy wooden boardwalks lead from six roadside parking areas through fragile dunes to ocean beach where low-tide walks are best. Much of the beach is closed during the piping plover nesting season.

Hellcat Interpretive Trail (a 1.4-mile self-guiding two-part trail: Marsh Trail and Dunes Trail) begins 3.5 miles south of the entrance and traverses freshwater marsh and upland woods, cresting at a 50-foot high dune with a fine panoramic view. Pines Trail (.3 mile) originates .65 mile beyond the Hellcat Parking Lot. The latter is accessible by wheelchair.

■ **PUBLICATIONS:** A list of refuge birds is available at the entrance station. Also available is a leaflet for Hellcat Interpretive Trail. A new general brochure is scheduled for publication in spring 2000.

Wapack NWR
Greenfield, New Hampshire

Conifers on rocky outcrop, Wapack NWR

As the only New England refuge to include a mountain summit within its borders, Wapack is unique. North Pack Monadnock is part of a range of mountains that rises like lone sentinels from the surrounding land. The spicy fragrance of spruce resin wafts in the air atop the mountain's gray granite-clad peak. On the grassy clearing of its windswept summit, the view suddenly and dramatically opens to reveal a world of rounded promontories and faint blue ridges stretching toward the horizon. En route to the top, in dimly lit forests that were once sunny pastures, shiny flecks of mica glisten within the rocks.

HISTORY

Native Americans once lived in and around these mountains. Until 1901, farmers drove cattle from Massachusetts farms for summer grazing on what was then open pasture extending nearly to the summit of both Pack Monadnock and North Pack Monadnock. (Pack Monadnock, two miles south of North Pack, is not within the refuge.) Still present are old rock walls, now curiously out of place in the spruce woods. The 1,672-acre refuge, established in 1972 and administered by Great Meadows NWR, serves about 4,000 visitors each year.

GETTING THERE

From Rte. 3 in Nashua, take Rte. 101A northwest for 9 mi. to Rte. 101 and follow it for about 16 mi. to Miller State Park on the right. The Wapack Trail and the refuge are accessible from the parking area just off the road.

■ **SEASON:** Refuge open year-round. Auto road to Pack Monadnock summit: summer and on spring and fall weekends. Miller State Park: Memorial Day weekend Labor Day.

■ **HOURS:** Refuge open dawn to dusk. Office (Great Meadows NWR): Mon.-Fri., 7:30 a.m.–4 p.m.

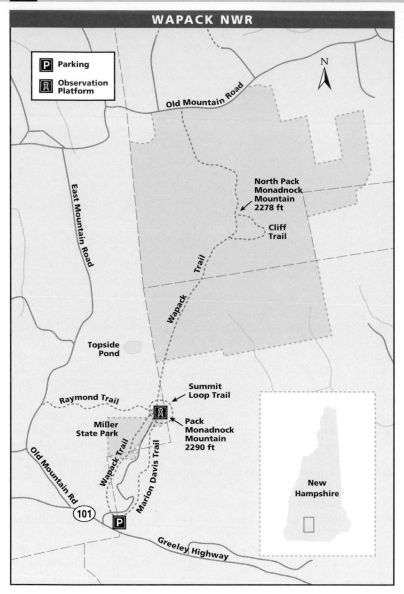

WAPACK NWR

Parking

Observation Platform

N

Old Mountain Road

East Mountain Road

North Pack Monadnock Mountain 2278 ft

Cliff Trail

Wapack Trail

Topside Pond

Raymond Trail

Summit Loop Trail

Miller State Park

Pack Monadnock Mountain 2290 ft

Wapack Trail

Marion Davis Trail

Old Mountain Rd

101

Greeley Highway

New Hampshire

■ **FEES:** Free access. Miller State Park: $2 per person; fee does not apply to through hikers unless you stop for lunch or for more than 15 minutes.

■ **ADDRESS:** Wapack NWR, c/o Great Meadows NWR, Weir Hill Road, Sudbury, MA 01776

■ **TELEPHONE, FAX, AND E-MAIL:** Great Meadows NWR: 978/443-4661; fax: 978-443-2898; e-mail: R5RW_GMNWR@fws.gov; Miller State Park: 978/924-9963

TOURING WAPACK

■ **BY AUTOMOBILE:** Not permitted on the refuge; you can drive to the summit of Pack Monadnock and hike from there.

■ **BY FOOT:** The refuge and vicinity are ideal for hikers. The 21-mile Wapack Trail, established in 1923, includes three miles on refuge property. A total of 13.5 miles of trails traverses the area, including four trail approaches to the summit of Pack Monadnock and two trails to North Pack Monadnock (2,278 feet).

■ **BY BICYCLE:** Not permitted on refuge property. You may ride up the winding 1.3-mile paved auto road to the top of Pack Monadnock or to where Wapack Trail meets Old Mountain Road (East Mountain Road on some maps) and proceed on foot from there.

■ **BY CANOE, KAYAK, OR BOAT:** Access not possible.

WHAT TO SEE

■ **LANDSCAPE AND CLIMATE** From the rocky, partly open summit of North Pack Monadnock, the views, especially to the south, of Pack Monadnock (2,290 feet), and west to Mount Monadnock (3,165 feet), are stunning. On a clear day you can see the Boston skyline, 55 miles to the south.

"Monadnock" is a geological term for a New England mountain, a lone resistant mass amid a matrix of softer, more easily eroded material. Smooth granite domes are all that remain of a once higher plain.

May is blackfly season. Summers are pleasingly cool, seldom exceeding 85 degrees. Fall is delightful for the foliage and hiking, while winters are cold and snowy, especially at upper elevations.

■ **PLANT LIFE**

Rocky summit and ledge The mountain's grassy balds—open meadowlike areas—are vegetated with fine-leafed clumps of the aptly named hair grass. The gray granite ledge, or bedrock, is draped with tight rosettes of gray-green lichens. The smallest wildflower of these virtually treeless summits is the three-toothed cinquefoil (note three teeth on each of three leaflets). Tiny white flowers highlight its 1.5-inch-tall mats; its foliage turns wine-red in late summer. Exposed balds are also dotted with small gray birches whose leaves have long tapered tips; pin or fire cherry thrives in the sunny openings as a small tree or shrub. Mountain ash, a lovely small tree with compound leaves and unpretentious white blossoms, produces heavy clusters of scarlet berries in late summer.

Meadowsweet shrubs bloom in midsummer with palm-sized bouquets of minute pink flowers at the tips of the branches. Red cedar attains only bush height on these rocks, while late lowbush, velvetleaf, and highbush blueberries all grow in profusion. Some ripen as early as July. Dense clumps of prickly dwarf or common juniper grow among the rock crevices. Wildlife consumes this evergreen's hard blue-black berries.

Northern hardwood forest Ninety percent of the refuge consists of timbered slopes where cattle grazed 100 years ago. Lower slopes are clothed in northern red oak, red maple, white and yellow birches (with brassy peeling bark), white pine, and red spruce. The forest floor in spots is covered by a thick growth of spruce seedlings; older trees attain 18 inches in diameter. Also populating the forest are smooth-trunked American beech, scaly-barked black cherry, and a few eastern hemlocks. Striped maple (aka moosewood, goosefoot maple), with its light-green striated bark, becomes common mid-story shrub.

Evergreen mountain laurel produces an ample bouquet of white to pink nickel-sized flowers in mid- to late June. Sheep laurel, its smaller relative, has light green leaves and smaller, pinker flowers. It is highly toxic and has been shown to poison livestock who eat its leaves. Among a half dozen common ferns you can spot here, watch for yellow-green hay-scented fern, which prefers old pastures and forms luxuriant growths. Common polypody is small and bound to boulders. Interrupted fern and cinnamon fern are quite similar, growing waist high, with cinnamon preferring wet roots. New York fern grows knee-high and tapers at both ends. Bracken is big and coarse, frequenting sunny spots and dry, sandy soils.

The woodland floor is made more enchanting by four species of club moss. Their names are descriptive: ground cedar, shining clubmoss, princess pine (which most resembles a Lilliputian tree), and staghorn clubmoss (which resembles the fuzzy summer antlers of deer). All spread slowly from shallow runners and reproduce by means of spores.

Under oaks and pines an acidic humus predominates, favoring such familiar spring wildflowers as starflower (white blossoms), Canada mayflower, Clintonia (aka bluebead lily), and wild sarsaparilla with three small white globular flower heads. Pink lady's slipper, a common orchid of southern New England, blooms in June. In late summer whorled wood aster brightens the forest. It displays white flowers at the top of a one- to three-foot stem.

Evergreen forest On the upper slopes, dense stands of young and middle-aged red spruce hold sway. Look for silvery-green mounds of attractive white cushion moss on acid soils, especially under spruces. Haircap moss, bushier and darker green, is familiar on moist soils worldwide. In low-lying pockets of saturated soils, the peat-forming, yellow-green sphagnum mosses predominate.

Wood sorrel

Delicate wood sorrel (*Oxalis*), with shamrocklike leaves, grows in shaded damp soils, its petals traced with fine pink lines in midsummer. Indian cucumber root has an edible root the size of your pinkie finger and puts out nice greenish-yellow flowers above the second whorl of leaves. Bunchberry, a dwarf dogwood only several inches high, forms coral red berries in late summer. Partridgeberry creeps with small paired leaves and white trumpet-shaped flowers. Wintergreen has shiny, dark green leaves year-round and produces edible red berries. Goldthread also has shiny, dark-green leaves, as well as starry white blossoms, and takes its name from its roots.

■ ANIMAL LIFE

Birds In the northern hardwoods, watch and listen for black-throated blue warbler (*beer-beer-bee*); blue-headed vireo; hermit thrush, one of North America's premier songsters; the carpenter ant-loving pileated woodpecker; and the dainty red-breasted nuthatch, which has a higher, more nasal call than its larger cousin. Ruffed grouse generally depend on their cryptic coloration to avoid detection, but a hen partridge with a brood of chicks can be very animated in their defense. One may charge, head down, directly toward you, making odd mewing sounds. The object is to turn your attention from her chicks. It usually works.

On the upper slopes and summits nest the yellow-rumped warbler, which also has yellow on its flanks and on top of its head; the lovely magnolia warbler; the winter wren, one of the loudest singers for its size; white-throated sparrows, whose plaintive *old Sam Peabody, Peabody, Peabody* song is beloved by many; and the diminutive golden-crowned kinglet, often seen hovering among the spruce boughs in search of insects.

Swainson's thrush, a diminishing species, also breeds in these cool woodlands. The gray and white dark-eyed junco lays its eggs on the ground in the summit area. Some autumns, flocks of chunky yellow, black, and white evening grosbeaks wander down from more northern latitudes and some stay to raise young.

Occasionally a true northerner, such as boreal chickadee, may show up. Be alert for its nasal *chick-che-day-day* song.

Yellow-rumped warbler bathing

In summer, flocks of fruit-eating, fly-catching cedar waxwings move about in search of food, while blue-green tree swallows wheel over the summit, feeding on flying insects. Indigo buntings, gorgeous bright blue finches that require open spaces, frequent the grassy balds. Be sure to gaze skyward for hawks soaring overhead. But if the bird is big, black, and rocking on the wind, it is probably a turkey vulture.

Mammals Moose sometimes wander into the area. These are often young bulls seeking a territory to call their own. Lightning-fast long-tailed weasels prey on deer mice and birds. Gray foxes, which climb trees, enjoy fruit in late summer, and bobcats, which prefer rocky ledges, include mice, voles, squirrels, and snowshoe hares in their diets. The hares have huge hind feet that enable them to travel through deep snow with relative ease. Black bears are sometimes reported, and raccoons are common; both are omnivorous.

Reptiles and amphibians Garter and smooth green snakes, after basking on the sun-warmed granite, seek out toads, sluggish insects, and other fare on the summits. Two species of frog often found far from water may cross your path.

American toads can store large amounts of liquid within their bodies, and their thick, warty skins allow them to live high and dry. Wood frogs, as their name implies, are found in forests. These black-masked amphibians must lay their eggs in woodland ponds, called vernal pools, in early spring. Slender red-backed salamanders spend their days under the cover of fallen logs in the hardwood forest and usually escape notice.

View of Mt. Monadnock from top of Wapack NWR

Invertebrates In May, biting blackflies, minute hunch-backed insects, torment humans and wildlife alike, while in June, female deer flies, which also inflict painful bites, seek their blood meals.

The most obvious insect during summer is the large green darner dragonfly; on the sunny summit of North Pack Monadnock, the air is sometimes filled with these insects, darting about, hovering, and snatching prey in midair. These swift fliers have two distinct populations in the east. One generation drifts northward in spring from breeding areas in the southern United States. In fall, their offspring move southward along the coast in huge congregations to southern states where they breed, completing the cycle.

ACTIVITIES

■ **CAMPING:** Camping is not permitted. The nearest public campground is at Greenfield State Park, 603/547-3497. Camping is allowed at Monadnock State Park, 603/532-8862, where more primitive conditions prevail.

■ **WILDLIFE OBSERVATION:** Colorful wood warblers, evening grosbeak, Swainson's thrush, and other northern specialties make Wapack an enjoyable birding location. Large mammals including black bear and moose are sometimes reported from the refuge or Miller State Park.

Hawk-watching from the summit of either peak in fall is arguably the most spectacular wildlife event of the year, especially if winds are brisk and out of the northwest. In September and October, the summits are good places from which to spot southbound broad-winged, sharp-shinned, and red-tailed hawks.

■ **PHOTOGRAPHY:** Panoramic vistas on clear days are sublime. Mount Monadnock, 12 miles west, is best photographed during morning, with the sun at your back. You may wish to use a polarizing filter, and a skylight filter for haze is almost a must. Woodlands wildflowers make lovely subjects in May and June. Given that it is often dark in the forest, even at midday, a tripod is helpful, as is fast film.

■ **HIKES AND WALKS:** Hiking is decidedly up and down, although the approach from the Rte. 101 parking lot over the Wapack Trail to the Pack Monadnock summit (2,290 feet) was made safer and more gradual in 1998. If planning to hike from the highway to Old Mountain Road and back, allow eight hours. Beginning and ending at the parking lot on the Pack Monadnock summit can reduce the time by at least two hours.

From the parking lot off Rte. 101, choose either the yellow-blazed Wapack Trail or blue-blazed Marion Davis Trail, each 1.4 miles, to the summit of Pack Monadnock (elevation gain 800 feet, allow one hour). Beginning the hike from the summit saves 2.8 round-trip miles. Even so, it is still a total of eight moderately strenuous miles to Old Mountain Road and back.

From the busy summit of Pack Monadnock (restrooms, picnic tables, water fountain), the unmarked refuge boundary, at about the low point on the trail, lies about .5 miles to the north. Allow 1.5 hours from Pack Monadnock to the undeveloped summit of North Pack Monadnock (2,278 feet, another 600-foot eleva-

HUNTING AND FISHING
Not permitted on the refuge.

tion gain after descending Pack Monadnock) and an additional hour to Old Mountain Road.

A distinctly shorter route is south from Old Mountain Road on the Wapack Trail for 1.5 miles to North Pack Monadnock. Cliff Trail is a 1.2-mile loop extension on North Pack, which you may want to walk if time permits.

All trails are well-marked and maintained by Friends of the Wapack, local volunteers. In winter, snowshoes and cross-country skis come in handy.

■ **PUBLICATIONS:** "Wapack Trail Guide," by John E. Flanders, is available from Friends of the Wapack, P.O. Box 115, West Peterborough, NH 03468.

Block Island NWR
New Shoreham, Rhode Island

Dusty miller at foot of the dunes, Block Island NWR

With green pastures, gray stone walls, and elegant Victorian homes, Block Island welcomes visitors. Sandy beaches, bathed by the surf, and sweeping dunes constitute the refuge at the island's windswept northern tip. North Light stands stalwart, adjacent to the refuge. Established in 1973 and administered by Ninigret NWR, the refuge occupies a former U.S. Coast Guard light station.

GETTING THERE

Block Island is 12 mi. off the Rhode Island coast. Ferries leave from Point Judith, RI, off Rte. 108 (year-round; cars by reservation only, 401-783-4613). Seasonal ferries also depart from Newport and Narragansett, RI, New London, CT, and Montauk, NY. Commercial flights also available.

   Once on the island, drive or pedal northward on Corn Neck Road for about 4 mi. to end of pavement.

■ **SEASON:** Refuge open year-round.

■ **HOURS:** Refuge: Dawn to dusk. North Light Interpretive Center: Weekends, Memorial Day to Columbus Day and daily from late June to mid-Sept., 10 a.m.–5 p.m.

■ **FEES:** Free access; admission fee for interpretive center.

■ **ADDRESS:** Block Island NWR, c/o Ninigret NWR, P. O. Box 307, Charlestown, RI 02813.

■ **TELEPHONE, FAX, AND E-MAIL:** Ninigret NWR: 401/364-9124; fax: 401/364-0170; e-mail: R5RW_NINWR@fws.gov; North Light Interpretive Center: 401/466-3220

TOURING BLOCK ISLAND

■ **BY FOOT** Parking area to North Light is .5 mile. From lighthouse to tip of Sandy Point (off refuge property) is .4 mile (some walking through loose sand).

You may also walk the .5 mile of refuge beach from the lighthouse (one-way). The island has an extensive Greenway Trails network.

WHAT TO SEE

Block Island, Long Island, Martha's Vineyard, and Nantucket mark the southernmost advance of a glacier 12,000 years ago. Sand, gravel, and boulders are the surviving evidence of the ice sheet. Sandy Point, at the mercy of the elements and without trees, is often a bright, sunny place. Dunes 40 feet high are covered with a thick shrubby growth.

American beach grass, the master dune builder, creates habitat for insects, rodents, and other wildlife. The dunes also harbor beach pea, dusty miller (an alien relative of sagebrush), and saltspray rose, a lovely exotic with palm-sized white flowers and fat rose hips. In late summer the dunes glow with the golden hues of seaside goldenrod.

Between dunes, thickets of beach plum, bayberry, poison ivy, and winterberry produce fruits consumed by birds and mammals; the head-high shrubs also provide shade, shelter, resting, and nest sites for wildlife. Tree swallows by the thousands fatten up on the bayberry fruits in autumn, and yellow-rumped warblers, which nest in northern and mountainous portions of New England, winter in abundance.

This critical stopover point for migrant birds is also home to nesting species linked largely to the sea. Most common are great black backed and herring gulls, with smaller numbers of black-headed laughing gulls. In winter, look for the common loon, northern gannet, great cormorant, common eider, white-winged scoter, common goldeneye, and red-breasted merganser offshore. Be alert for harbor and gray seals in winter.

Great blue heron, belted kingfisher, black crowned night heron, and northern harrier frequent freshwater wetlands. Statuesque mute swans, European imports, may be upsetting the ecological balance of Sachem Pond. Snapping turtles also dwell in the pond, and garter snakes hunt there for frogs, fish, and insects.

Surf scoter

Look for the tracks of the common white-tailed deer along the muddy pond shores. Abundant meadow voles— brown short-tailed field mice that build runways through the thatch—are high on the menu of most predators. Alert visitors may also see the diminutive masked shrew, migrating red bat, and familiar striped skunk.

In summer, big-headed green darner dragonflies patrol the skies while bumblebees and honeybees collect nectar and pollen from goldenrod and other blossoms. Flip over a board or other piece of debris and you may see amphipods such as beach fleas hopping about. Scores of monarch butterflies can be seen during their annual southbound migrations, September to early October. Meanwhile, peregrine falcons and merlins pick off avian stragglers.

Just offshore, lobsters are the quarry of humans; bright-colored plastic floats mark traps set for them. Blue crabs, green crabs, lady or calico crabs, and long-legged spider crabs inhabit intertidal and deeper waters. Periwinkles, which scrape algae off rocks with filelike tongues, are revealed by a falling tide.

■ **WILDLIFE OBSERVATION:** Find shorebirds, gulls, terns, and other marine life by walking along Cow Cove beach to the tip of Sandy Point, then southward along the strand bordering Block Island Sound. In spring and summer, do not disturb their nesting activities. In September and October, after northwest winds cause what's known as a fallout, bushes may resemble living Christmas trees decorated with warblers, vireos, flycatchers, and kinglets.

Gaze skyward for migrating hawks and monarch butterflies in late summer and early fall. The best birding-for ducks, geese, swans, cormorants, and herons-adjacent to the refuge is along the north shore of 105-acre Sachem Pond.

■ **HIKES AND WALKS:** Walking from the parking area to North Light and on to the tip of Sandy Point and back by way of Block Island Sound beach covers about 1.7 miles. To see more of the refuge, turn right after you leave the lighthouse, proceed through the gap in the dune, and turn left down the beach. The refuge boundary extends almost .5 miles south. Do not attempt to cross the dunes; shortcutting harms vegetation, and the thick shrubbery, including poison ivy, is virtually impassable.

■ **PUBLICATIONS:** Richard Bowen. "Nesting Birds of Block Island." Block Island Conservancy and Audubon Society of Rhode Island (1981).

Two brochures, "Wildlife Refuges of Rhode Island" and "Birds of the National Wildlife Refuges of Rhode Island," are available from the Ninigret NWR office.

Ninigret NWR
Charlestown, Rhode Island

A path to the ocean, Ninigret NWR

Encompassing fields, forest, shrubby thickets, freshwater ponds, and a small portion of Atlantic barrier beach adjacent to the largest coastal pond in Rhode Island, Ninigret offers wonderful wildlife viewing year-round and comparable facilities. Wide, level paths and wildlife observation platforms will make your visit to this former naval air station very enjoyable.

This is a fine place to witness the healing powers of nature. What were once paved runways are now reverting to shrublands as insistent woody plants exploit each nook and cranny in the old pavement, forcing their probing roots deep into the soil beneath. In time, the vestiges of human occupation will be totally eliminated. But Ninigret is already one of the finest locales for wildlife observation in coastal Rhode Island.

HISTORY

A U.S. naval air station was built on this site in 1940, and was later decommissioned. The refuge and five other properties in the complex were established during the early to mid-1970s, but signs of its former use are still very evident. Former runways, now overgrown, serve as broad level trails, and even a pair of old runway markers are still in place along Grassy Point Trail. The 400-acre refuge is named for a chief of the Niantic people who lived along the western Rhode Island and eastern Connecticut coast. Fifteen thousand people visit annually.

GETTING THERE

Two public entrances are located very close together. To reach the east entrance when driving west from Charlestown, follow Rte. 1A to Ninigret Park (Rte. 1 and Rte. 1A converge between east and west entrance roads). The east entrance road is .5 mi. east of the Rte. 1/Rte. 1A merge. This entrance leads first to Ninigret Park

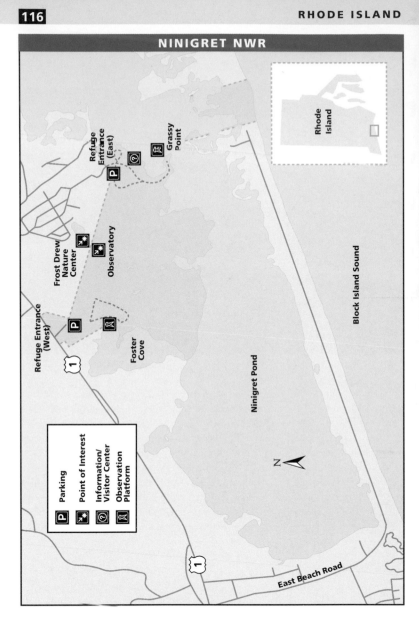

NINIGRET NWR

Public Recreation Area and Frosty Drew Nature Center, both owned and operated by the Town of Charlestown.

To reach the west entrance, continue west on Rte. 1, after the Rte. 1/Rte. 1A convergence, a short distance to the next street on the left. Both entrances are well marked.

■ **SEASON:** Refuge open year-round; barrier beach area closed to vehicles during piping plover nesting season, April.-Aug.

■ **HOURS:** Refuge open dawn to dusk; headquarters in Charlestown is open Mon.–Fri., 8 a.m.–4:30 p.m. Frosty Drew Nature Center open Tues.–Sun., 10 a.m.–5 p.m.; closed Mon.

■ **FEES:** Free access to refuge and Frosty Drew Nature Center.

■ **ADDRESS:** Ninigret National Wildlife Refuge, Box 307, Charlestown, RI 02813. Frosty Drew Nature Center, Ninigret Park Recreation Area, Box 160, Charlestown, RI 02813.
■ **TELEPHONE, FAX, AND E-MAIL:** Refuge Headquarters: 401/364-9124; fax: 401/364-0170; e-mail: R5RW_NINWR@fws.gov; Frosty Drew Nature Center: 401/364-9508

TOURING NINIGRET
■ **BY AUTOMOBILE:** The refuge is closed to vehicles.
■ **BY FOOT:** Two paths at the eastern and western sides of the property combine for a total of 2.5 miles of walking trails. It is not possible to cross refuge property from one trail to the other. A well-maintained chemical toilet is at the west entrance parking area.
■ **BY BICYCLE:** Bicycling is not permitted on refuge property, but you may ride on the adjacent Ninigret Park Recreation Area.
■ **BY CANOE, KAYAK, OR BOAT:** Boating is popular on 1,700-acre Ninigret Pond with its access to the Atlantic (a narrow human-engineered breachway), but it is not a good way to access the property, except for the small portion of barrier beach that is part of the smaller, outer section of the refuge.

WHAT TO SEE
■ **LANDSCAPE AND CLIMATE**
Ninigret presents a bucolic scene with an open, sunny disposition. Nature is rapidly reclaiming the tarmac and other signs of past human disturbance. This flat coastal land is bathed in nearly constant breezes that, in combination with sandy soils and bright sun, have given rise to profuse shrub thickets festooned with climbing vines of oriental bittersweet and wild grape.

Grassy Point, at the narrow entrance to Ninigret Pond, is an especially picturesque, windswept location that affords wonderful views from an observation platform. Granite boulders, remnants of retreating glacial ice some 10,000 to 12,000 years ago, dot the shoreline. Compared with the inland New England climate, conditions are relatively mild, with temperatures seldom dropping below 20 degrees F in winter.

■ **PLANT LIFE**
Coastal scrub Some three decades after the abandonment of the naval air station, refuge vegetation is still regenerating. Arrowwood; shining or winged sumac (both descriptive names); smooth sumac, which lacks the fuzzy twigs of staghorn sumac; and the alien Tartarian honeysuckle, a prolific producer of translucent red berries, are all abundant. Other shrubs include highbush blueberry, red raspberry, blackberry, and sweet pepperbush, whose fragrant white flowers appear in summer. Chokeberry, a relative of the domestic apple, resembles Juneberry, but has tiny glands on the midrib of its leaves that you will need a hand lens to see. Oblong-leaf Juneberry or shad thrives in the woody thickets.

Multiflora rose was planted for decades for erosion control and as wildlife food and cover benefits during the mid-20th century. It is now looked on as an invasive exotic, its positive contributions notwithstanding. Russian olive was planted for similar reasons. The silvery, linear leaves are especially visible when set in motion by the wind. It is among the few nonlegumes that fix atmospheric nitrogen in the soil by means of bacterial root nodules.

Oriental bittersweet insidiously sends its twining woody stems up trees and shrubs, eventually choking off the plant's circulation. Native wild grape and poison ivy are common also; all three provide food for birds and are distributed by birds and, in the case of grapes, by mammals as well. Common dodder, an unusual parasitic plant that looks like thin orange spaghetti draped over shrubbery, absorbs the sap of its host plants through tiny suckers.

In sandy soils near Ninigret Pond, big saltspray *(Rugosa)* rosebushes produce impressive pink flowers in midsummer. Later this nonnative yields oversized red rose hips, while beach pea, a dune plant, spreads along the ground in the sandy glacial soils.

Old fields Perhaps the most abundant grass in this open landscape is little bluestem. The shrub meadowsweet has large clusters of small pinkish-white flowers in midsummer. You cannot fail to notice yellow-blooming goldenrods, including the lovely seaside goldenrod; the familiar black-eyed Susan; common milkweed; Saint-John's-wort; butterfly pea, a twining plant that produces showy pale-blue flowers; and black knapweed. Knapweed's blossoms faintly resemble those of thistles; it is one of the most abundant late summer wildflowers along the trails.

Colonizers of open ground, such as red cedar, black cherry, and white pine, represent an early stage in the regeneration of the area's woodlands. All require significant sunlight and will be replaced in the future by shade-tolerant trees, such as oaks. Red cedar and black cherry develop summer fruits readily eaten by birds and mammals. The hard "berries" of red cedar gave cedar waxwings at least a portion of their name, and they contribute a distinctive flavor to gin.

Woodland Few large trees are to be found at Ninigret. The red maple's foliage turns a flaming scarlet in fall. Other trees include white oak (whose leaves have rounded lobes) and red oak (pointed lobes). The quaking aspen also requires considerable sun. European larch grows along the edge of the airstrip, where they were planted.

In the semishade and moist situations in the open woods, you will find the unmistakable jack-in-the-pulpit, impressive orange flowers of Turk's cap lily, the unpretentious enchanter's nightshade, and jewelweed, whose orange trumpet-shaped blossoms are a favorite of hummingbirds. Pokeweed grows to 10 feet in height and produces clusters of large purple-black berries with red stalks that can be poisonous to humans. The young shoots, however, are sometimes eaten, especially in the South.

Freshwater wetlands The surface of a small freshwater pond near the shore of Ninigret Pond is covered in summer with floating mats of yellow-green algae, among the most primitive plants. The algae's decay gives off sulfurous odors. Common reed *(Phragmites)* produces large purplish plumes in late summer. This invasive has limited wildlife value and threatens to squeeze out more valuable species. Speckled alder, dominant in shrub swamps, produces small conelike fruiting bodies.

In mucky soils the large pink-topped clumps of joe-pye weed, tall meadow rue, and boneset, once used for its medicinal qualities, are common. Magenta-flowered swamp loosestrife, unlike the invasive purple loosestrife, is a native species. Sensitive and cinnamon ferns require moist or saturated soils; cinnamon's fertile fronds, which produce the spores, are long and tawny.

Salt marshes Along the shores of brackish Ninigret Pond, salt-meadow cord grass has thin stems and very narrow leaves. Freshwater cordgrass, a much more robust species, grows on somewhat drier sites near the pond.

■ ANIMAL LIFE

Birds White-eyed vireo, a bird of the tangles, is virtually unknown north of coastal New England. You will probably hear its sharp *chick-a-perweeoo-chick* song before you see one. Carolina wrens, in contrast, sing an upbeat, loud *teakettle, teakettle, teakettle* song from the shrubbery.

Look for double-crested cormorants on the waters of Foster Cove. The snowy egret, the larger great egret (orange bill), the crow-sized green heron, and the American bittern—a cryptically colored two-foot-tall bird that spends most daylight hours in dense vegetation—all frequent the margins of ponds. Each employs a different method of feeding, thereby avoiding competition.

The pond itself is a haven for waterfowl. The most common is American black duck. Because the salty waters do not freeze, many other species are present in fall and winter. Nesting ospreys dive into Ninigret Pond for fish.

The large number of alien mute swans, the familiar park variety, can have quite a negative impact. They foul the water with excrement, aggressively displace native waterfowl, and consume vast quantities of aquatic plants.

The tiny threatened least tern nests on the sandy stretches of the barrier beach, as does the threatened piping plover; the beach is closed during the breeding season. In late summer, look also for the larger Forster's tern, identified after the breeding season by a black streak through the eye region; it nests in inland marshes.

In late summer, plovers and sandpipers come to feed and rest during migratory periods. Species vary weekly from late July through October; two of the most common are greater yellowlegs, one of the largest, and least sandpiper, the smallest. Stay alert too for migrant hawks.

Tree swallow on nest box

In arguably the greatest avian spectacle at Ninigret, tens of thousands of migrant tree swallows wheel over the salt marshes like a swarm of locusts. These winged creatures feed on flying insects and on nutritious waxy bayberries. Fattening up on their southward migration, they winter from the mid-Atlantic coast southward.

Winter visitors such as snowy owl and rough-legged hawk frequent the area during some years when their Arctic food supplies run short.

Reptiles and amphibians Painted turtles are seen often, given their habit of basking on logs, rocks, and other objects. Look for them at the small freshwater pond along the Grassy Point Trail. You may find remnants of their nests, dug up by raccoons, skunks, and other predators.

One of the smallest snakes, the reclusive northern brown, is usually less than one foot long. It has two parallel rows of blackish spots down the back, eats slugs, worms, and soft-bodied insects, and bears live young.

Look and listen for frogs at the small freshwater pond along the northeast portion of the Grassy Point Trail. The most abundant frog, the big bullfrog, sends out a familiar deep *jug-o-rum* call on warm late spring and summer days.

Mammals You might find the scat of coyote and its smaller cousin the red fox along refuge trails where these predators search for meadow voles, white-footed mice, and cottontail rabbits. The largest mammal is the beguiling white-tailed deer, although you will likely see only their tracks during daylight hours. The abundant berry-producing shrubs provide a bounty for such omnivorous creatures as raccoon, striped skunk, and opossum.

Fishes The brackish waters of Ninigret Pond support winter flounder, a "right-eyed" flatfish (adults average 15 inches and two pounds) that enters the pond in winter to spawn at night. Schools of young bluefish, a species popular with sport anglers, enter to feed during the summer months. The small baitfish species that this and other predatory fish feed on include white perch, mummichog, and silversides—all abundant species tolerant of brackish conditions.

Invertebrates In summer, colorful butterflies are numerous. An uncommon small butterfly this far north is the white M hairstreak; it takes its name from the white and black-bordered band in the shape of the letter M on the underside of its brownish hind wings.

Along the shores of the pond, look for smaller species such as slipper or boat shells, which have an interesting sex life. The sex of one animal is determined by the sex of those around it. A male remains male as long as it is attached to a female. Once a male becomes a female, however, it remains a female.

The tiny cone-shaped drills, as their name implies, drill into larger shellfish and eat the fleshy contents. You might also find an occasional horseshoe crab (not really a crab at all, but a predatory representative of an ancient group of arthropods). During the May full moon, egg-laden females come ashore to lay masses of small greenish eggs in the sand. The odds of the eggs reaching the hatching

Former pasture regenerating to red cedars, Ninigret NWR

stage are slim—they are at risk of being eagerly devoured by migrant shorebirds and resident gulls.

For a sample of the type of shellfish that live in Ninigret Pond, check the broken shells dropped by herring gulls on the old tarmac. Among the fragments you will find an abundance of thick-shelled quahog, bay scallop (ridged shells), oyster (irregular, rough shells), and several crab species—blue, the famous and highly edible crab of Chesapeake Bay; spider, named for its long, gangly legs; and Atlantic rock crab. This crab's front claws (pincers) are black.

ACTIVITIES

■ **SWIMMING AND CAMPING:** Swimming is not allowed anywhere on the refuge. Camping is not permitted on refuge property; the nearest public campground is the Burlington Camping Area, off Rte. 1.

■ **WILDLIFE OBSERVATION:** A well-maintained trail system, complete with observation platform, enhances wildlife viewing year-round; the platform near the tip of Grassy Point provides a wonderful vantage point from which to observe birds. A second platform is planned for the Foster Cove Trail.

■ **PHOTOGRAPHY:** Although this was a naval air station, Ninigret is a scenic place offering many photographic opportunities. The panoramic views from the Grassy Point observation platform are especially lovely. Butterflies make photogenic subjects, especially if you have a macro lens and tripod.

■ **HIKES AND WALKS:** If time is limited, walk the 1.4-mile (round-trip) trail to Grassy Point. A bench is situated where you can enjoy the shoreline of Ninigret Pond, and the obser-

> **HUNTING AND FISHING**
> Hunting is not permitted on refuge property, nor are firearms permitted. **Surf fishing** is permitted from refuge seashores under applicable state and federal regulations. For information on current license requirements, seasons, and limits, consult refuge office.

vation platform near the point is a great place to sit, relax, and enjoy the fine views. A picnic table is at the parking area.

Foster Cove Trail, accessible from the western entrance, is 1.1 miles in length and passes near the shore of Foster Cove. At present, access to the shore is poor—only a couple of overgrown paths down to the water's edge, where visibility is limited. The trail is wide and level and a picnic table and chemical toilet are at the parking area. An information board with map is at both entrances.

■ **SEASONAL EVENTS:** Interpretive programs are conducted by refuge staff at various locations throughout the year; call weekdays for information. The municipally operated Frosty Drew Nature Center offers additional public education programs at the refuge; contact the center for program information.

■ **PUBLICATIONS:** Two U.S. Fish & Wildlife Service brochures, "Wildlife Refuges of Rhode Island" and "Birds of the National Wildlife Refuges of Rhode Island," are available from the Ninigret refuge complex office.

Sachuest Point NWR
Middletown, Rhode Island

Goldenrods and rocky coastline, Sachuest Point NWR

Set upon an open, windswept bluff, Sachuest Point commands a rugged and rocky coastline. It offers spectacular views that rival any in southern New England. Meadows and shrub-covered headlands stand in stark contrast to the dark-gray boulder-strewn shores and islets at the edge of the sea. In the boiling water below, rafts of exquisitely patterned harlequin ducks bob on the waves, diving periodically to wrest blue mussels from the bottom, and twice daily hermit crabs crawl through tidal pools as the sea recedes.

HISTORY

Sachuest Point NWR was established in 1970 as a migratory bird refuge along the Atlantic flyway. It occupies part of a former U.S. naval communications station and remnants of paved roadways remain. The 242-acre refuge is administered by Ninigret NWR and visited by some 36,000 people annually.

GETTING THERE

From Rte. 1, take Rte. 138 east over Newport Bridge (toll) and follow it east onto Miantonomi Ave. for .6 mi. Continue east on Green End Ave. for 1.2 mi., then turn right onto Paradise Ave. Drive 1.3 mi. and turn left onto Hanging Rock Rd. Continue .3 mi., then bear right onto Sachuest Point Rd. and follow it 1.5 mi. to refuge parking area and Visitor Center.
■ **SEASON:** Refuge open year-round.
■ **HOURS:** Refuge open dawn to dusk. Visitor Center open weekends, 10 a.m.– 4 p.m. on variable schedule; contact Visitor Center for current schedule.
■ **FEES:** Free access
■ **ADDRESS:** Sachuest Point NWR, c/o Ninigret NWR, P.O. Box 307, Charlestown, RI 02813-0307.
■ **TELEPHONE, FAX, AND E-MAIL:** Visitor Center: 401/847-5511; Ninigret

NWR: 401/364-9124; fax: 401/364-0170 (Ninigret); e-mail: HYPERLINK mail to:R5RW_NINWR@fws.gov; R5RW_NINWR@fws.gov (Ninigret)

TOURING SACHUEST POINT

■ **BY AUTOMOBILE:** No auto access beyond the paved parking area. During summer, heavy traffic to nearby beaches may cause lengthy delays along refuge access roads.

■ **BY FOOT:** Three miles of trails provide access and afford excellent views of the entire refuge, including the scenic coastline. Several benches and observation platforms are strategically situated along the trails, making walking here a pleasure. The Visitor Center (the only one in a Rhode Island NWR) features exhibits, audiovisual programs, and clean, modern rest rooms, accessible to people with disabilities.

■ **BY BICYCLE:** Not permitted on refuge trails. Bicycles may be used on the paved point road to the parking lot.

■ **BY CANOE, KAYAK, OR BOAT:** Accessing the refuge by boat is not recommended because of numerous rocks. Kayaking is permitted at sandy Third Beach, adjacent to the refuge.

WHAT TO SEE

■ **LANDSCAPE AND CLIMATE** Shaped somewhat like a foot, the peninsula is bordered by Sachuest Bay on the west and the Sakonnet River on the east. Views are breathtaking, as few trees are present to obstruct your vision. Sandy beaches exist along Sachuest Point Rd. on your way to the parking area, but the persona of this refuge is certainly jagged and rocky. Here the weather can transform quickly and dramatically from breezy, cold, and damp, to warm, sunny, and dry, or vice versa. The coastline can be shrouded in fog, even in summer; fierce onshore winds during winter are often frigid and biting.

■ **PLANT LIFE**
Coastal shrubland The refuge is covered by a thick, almost impenetrable growth of high, shrubby vegetation. Bayberry thickets are quite substantial, with other common shrubs being arrowwood (long, straight branches); winterberry, whose fruits turn a bright red; and staghorn sumac (its branches resemble the fuzz-covered antlers of deer). One of the most attractive shrubs or small trees here is eastern wahoo or burning bush. Its characteristic four-lobed red fruits can be seen in early fall adjacent to the observation platform at Flint Point. The only real trees on the peninsula are some planted pines. Growth of the few red cedars has been stunted because of nearly constant buffeting by salt spray. In summer, saltspray or rugosa rosebushes display their numerous large pink blossoms.

The climbing vine oriental bittersweet is omnipresent. This exotic has draped itself literally everywhere and threatens to overcome the native vegetation. The skins of its yellow berries split open in early fall to reveal bright red berries, eaten by many songbirds. Another alien species, this one introduced intentionally for erosion control, is autumn olive. Its red berries are consumed by birds and mammals. Within the shrubby growth are other exotic plants, including multiflora rose, a white flowering plant that produces thorny tangles favored by mocking birds; and honeysuckle and crab apple, whose fruits are eaten by many birds. Poison ivy, another berry-producing climbing vine, or stand-alone bush, is also common. In fall its three-parted leaves turn shades of yellow and orange.

Meadows Sunny openings among the shrubs permit wildflowers and switchgrass to flourish. The meadows contain plants that testify to the soil's alteration by human activity, which has enabled alien species to dominate. Black knapweed, with thistlelike pink flowers, provides a favored nectar source for migrant monarch butterflies. Other exotics include the familiar Queen Anne's lace; butter-and-eggs (orange-and-yellow snapdragonlike flowers): yarrow; the sticky and fragrant night-flowering catchfly; common tansy, whose yellow rayless flowers look as though all their petals had been pulled off; bittersweet nightshade, which has ruby-red fruits; and various thistles.

In late summer, look also for New England aster, sporting large purplish blossoms, and small-flowered white aster, a common bushy plant here. The most common goldenrod in the sandy soils is the fragrant slender-leaved goldenrod.

Freshwater wetland Tall common reed (*Phragmites*) grows in thick stands in freshwater wetlands such as those near Third Beach. This huge grass is an invasive that crowds out other plants more beneficial to wildlife. Refuge staff regularly cut and treat the canes in an effort to control its spread.

Sandy beach and dunes Attractive seaside goldenrod, which has rather wide fleshy leaves, grows near the shore and is one of the few species able to colonize the shifting sands. The bright yellow flowers yield fat-rich nectar—food for migrant monarchs and other insects.

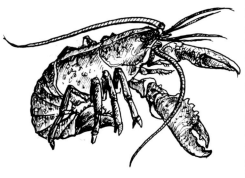

Northern lobster

Intertidal zone Growing between high and low tides and in deeper water are such "seaweeds" as kelp, rockweed, Irish moss, and green fleece, the spongy green import from Asia. Great quantities of long brown kelp fronds and masses of lacy Irish moss wash up on the cobble beaches of the eastern side of the point. Look for bright-green sea lettuce, an edible seaweed, in tidal pools at low tide.

■ ANIMAL LIFE

Birds Sachuest Point provides feeding, resting, and nesting habitat for numerous migratory birds; more than 200 species have been recorded. For birders, the winter months bring the most sought-after species. Harlequin ducks nest along turbulent mountain streams and cold Arctic shores, but winter along rocky coastlines as far south as Long Island. The wintering population here is the second largest in New England. Scan the Island Rocks for great cormorants, which have a white patch on the flank; several species of gulls, including the dainty Bonaparte's; and purple sandpipers, which are partial to rocks. Check ocean waters for common loon, common eider (the males are boldly patterned in black and white), and several species of scoters. Eiders, scoters, and harlequin ducks are all fond of blue mussels. From November through March you might even spy a short-eared owl or a big snowy owl.

Shrubby tangles provide nesting sites for birds that require semi-open habitats: eastern towhees can be heard uttering their scratchy *drink your tea* refrain, and song sparrows, catbirds, and their relatives the mockingbirds are common

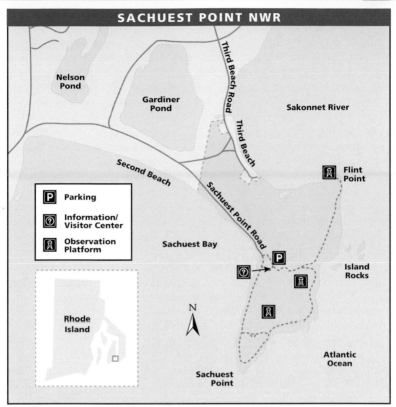

SACHUEST POINT NWR

Nelson Pond

Gardiner Pond

Third Beach Road

Third Beach

Sakonnet River

Second Beach

Sachuest Point Road

P Parking

ⓘ Information/ Visitor Center

Ⓧ Observation Platform

Sachuest Bay

Flint Point

Island Rocks

Rhode Island

N

Atlantic Ocean

Sachuest Point

too. Eastern phoebes (their song sounds like *fee-bee*) sit and wait for passing insects, which they capture in flight. You are also likely to hear the attention-getting *teakettle, teakettle, teakettle* offering of the Carolina wren. Common yellowthroat, the black-masked warbler, nests in wetland areas; offshore on the small islands, safe from predators, common terns raise their chicks.

Be on the lookout for hawks, shorebirds, and a variety of land birds during migration. Tree swallows by the thousands darken the skies over the refuge, fattening up on nutritious bayberries before their southward migration. Their locustlike flocks are quite a sight! They also nest in the fields in boxes that have been provided for them. Check the shrubbery for warblers, especially yellow-rumped, and American redstart. In late summer and early fall, black-bellied plovers, yellowlegs, and piebald ruddy turnstones (on the rocks) are fairly common transients. Look skyward for peregrine falcons and merlins, whose main fare is shorebirds.

Mammals Meadow voles, as is their lot, are a major food item in the diets of red fox, northern harrier, short-eared owl, rough-legged hawk, and—when they make a rare winter visit—snowy owls. The voles build an elaborate network of runways through the grassy thatch and multiply at a rapid rate. White-footed mice, warm brown above and white below, are numerous in the brushy areas. Eastern cottontails nibble on succulent (spring and summer) and woody (fall and winter) vegetation. Both rabbits and foxes, their predators, may be seen from the trails, especially early or late in the day. Striped skunks forage for insects and berries after nightfall. Although more frequently found farther up the coast, an occasional harbor seal winters on the rocks just offshore.

Invertebrates In early fall the most conspicuous insect is the large orange-and-black monarch butterfly. These powerful flyers average 40 miles a day on their southward migration along the coastline to central Mexico. Hundreds may pass by in a matter of hours, and many pause to draw nectar from knapweed flowers. Other common butterflies are cabbage white, an import, and clouded sulphur.

You will hear crickets chirping (they actually rub their wings together, not their legs) and see dragonflies, which are adept aerial hunters who pursue and capture insects in flight. You might come upon fuzzy brown-and-black-striped woolly bear caterpillars on the paths, especially in autumn. These Isabella moth larvae overwinter as caterpillars. Contrary to popular belief, the width of its brown band does not foretell the severity of the coming winter.

A crustacean of considerable commercial value is the lobster. Floats of baited lobster traps, called pots, dot the surface of the water just off the rocky shore. Lobsters are declining in population for several reasons, not the least of which is overfishing. Walk the beaches and you will find the remains of blue mussels, a favorite of some sea ducks, and small white-shelled dog whelks (when living, they drill into other shellfish with a filelike tongue and eat the contents). Among the less common shellfish are wavy astarte and quahog. A display inside the Visitor Center identifies much of what one will find on the beaches here.

One of the most intriguing and appealing creatures of the shore, the hermit crab, grows no protective shell of its own and so must seek out the empty shells of periwinkles and dog whelks. As the crab grows, it must periodically discard its home and find a new, roomier shell. You can find hermit crabs in tidepools among the rocks, left behind by a falling tide. The common species here is the long-clawed hermit. In this intertidal zone you will also see barnacles cemented to the rocks. Protected from dehydration by their tightly interlocking plates, barnacles wave feathery appendages to gather food—while standing on their heads! Other tidal-pool inhabitants include tiny green crabs and conical periwinkles.

> **HUNTING AND FISHING**
> Firearms are not permitted on refuge property. **Surf-fishing** is permitted from refuge seashores under applicable state and federal regulations. For information on current license requirements, seasons, and bag limits, consult refuge office.

Fishes Among the saltwater predatory game fish are bluefish, striped bass ("stripers"), and tautog (blackfish), which remain in these waters until December. Tautog have evolved heavy jaws for crushing shellfish. Bluefish and striped bass move to warmer waters in fall and are eagerly sought by surf fishermen then. In spring, as the sea warms, the fish move back into these waters. Bluefish, which often reach 10 or 12 pounds, have a formidable set of teeth. As adults they feed largely on squid and other fishes. Both breed in protected coastal estuaries, as do many other important saltwater species.

ACTIVITIES

■ **SWIMMING AND CAMPING:** Second (Sachuest) Beach and Third Beach, just off refuge property, are very popular for swimming in summer; both have a parking fee. Camping is not permitted on refuge property; the nearest campground is at Meadowlark RV Park (401-846-9455) on Aquidneck Island about two miles away.

Harlequin ducks

■ **WILDLIFE OBSERVATION:** Sachuest's fine trail system, three observation platforms, and absence of trees make for rather optimal wildlife viewing. You can easily scan the rocky shoreline and the shrubby interior from the trails; the middle observation platform provides a 360-degree view. Dozens of small, boldly colored male harlequin ducks and the drabber females can often be seen off the peninsula's eastern side from early November into March. A spotting scope helps here as at other coastal locations. With one, your chances of picking out (and identifying) far-off ducks, loons, grebes, and plunge-diving northern gannets are much improved.

■ **PHOTOGRAPHY:** Its small size notwithstanding, this refuge is one of the most scenic along the entire New England coast, offering a sublime coastal panorama. A most scenic view awaits visitors from the observation platform at Flint Point. The pounding surf and jagged gray rocks of Sachuest Point are wonderful subjects for the camera, as are butterflies alighting on wildflowers or fields of yellow goldenrods and red rose hips. Afternoon light illuminates the east shoreline after storm clouds lift, and a veil of fog weaves its own magic spell.

■ **HIKES AND WALKS:** Three miles of well-maintained broad and relatively level trails wind through the middle of the peninsula and along the shore. Several benches, offering fine views, are situated along the way, and three slightly elevated observation platforms provide panoramic vistas. Trails lead south to rocky Sachuest Point, and one leads north to Flint Point. All are on top of the bluff; none descend to the water's edge.

■ **SEASONAL EVENTS:** Guided interpretive programs, such as plant identification walks, are conducted periodically; contact the Visitor Center for information.

■ **PUBLICATIONS:** *Bird Walks in Rhode Island. Exploring the Ocean State's Best Sanctuaries,* by Adam R. Fry (1992); Backcountry Publications. Two brochures, "National Wildlife Refuges of Rhode Island" and "Birds of Sachuest Point National Wildlife Refuge," are available from the Visitor Center and from Ninigret NWR.

Trustom Pond NWR
South Kingstown, Rhode Island

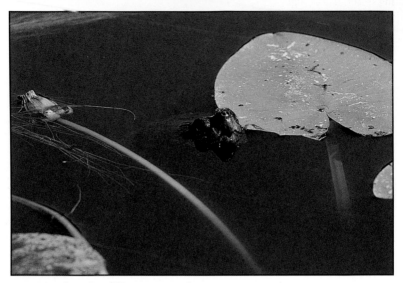

Snapping turtle amid pond lilies, Trustom Pond NWR

Trustom Pond is the only coastal pond in Rhode Island that remains free of development. As more and more of the surrounding coastal landscape is lost to construction and commercial activity, the existence of this bucolic landscape and the two other coastal Rhode Island refuges becomes critical to the welfare of many different living things. The 160-acre pond is separated from the sea by only a narrow strip of sandy barrier beach. The remaining landscape is one of gently rolling terrain, open fields, stone walls, low woods—or perhaps more accurately, tall shrubs—and lush farm ponds.

HISTORY

This 642-acre refuge was established in 1974 by private donation in order to provide important resting, feeding, and nesting habitat for migratory birds. A large portion of the refuge was once farmed, and evidence of agricultural practices is still present today.

On January 19, 1996, the barge *North Cape* ran aground off Moonstone Beach, spilling 828,000 gallons of home heating oil. Despite efforts to protect coastal ponds from contamination, Trustom, Ninigret, and Point Judith ponds were affected. And although tens of thousands of lobsters, shellfish, and crabs and hundreds of seabirds and other wildlife succumbed during the disaster, Trustom Pond apparently fared better than first feared. Then again, the long-range effects may not be fully known for decades.

The refuge, which receives 30,000 visitors yearly, is administered by Ninigret NWR, three miles west along the coast.

GETTING THERE

From Rte. 1 in South Kingstown, take the Moonstone Beach exit (which comes up rather suddenly) south for 1 mi. and then turn right onto Matunuck

Schoolhouse Rd. Continue for .7 mi. to the refuge entrance and parking on the left.

■ **SEASON:** Refuge open year-round; beach closed during piping plover nesting season, April–Aug.

■ **HOURS:** Refuge open dawn to dusk. Ninigret NWR office open weekdays from 8 a.m.–4:30 p.m.

■ **FEES:** Free access to refuge.

■ **ADDRESS:** Trustom Pond NWR, c/o Ninigret NWR, P.O. Box 307, Charlestown, RI 02813.

■ **TELEPHONE, FAX, AND E-MAIL:** 401/364-9124 (Ninigret NWR); fax: 401/364-0170; e-mail: R5RW_NINWR@fws.gov

TOURING TRUSTOM POND

■ **BY AUTOMOBILE:** Not accessible beyond entrance parking area. Parking limited to three hours. Barrier beach closed to vehicles during piping plover nesting season.

■ **BY FOOT:** Three miles of wide, gently sloping foot trails have been laid out in the north central part of the refuge and lead south to two observation platforms overlooking lovely Trustom Pond.

■ **BY BICYCLE:** Not permitted on refuge property.

■ **BY CANOE, KAYAK, OR BOAT:** It is possible to land on Moonstone Beach during fair-weather conditions.

WHAT TO SEE

■ **LANDSCAPE AND CLIMATE** The last glacier known to have visited Rhode Island some 10,000 to 12,000 years ago abruptly died just one mile north of Trustom Pond (north side of Rte. 1). Glacial till and outwash, the sand and gravel left by decaying ice, built the refuge's soils and gave rise to today's landscape. The sand-plain landscape is open and sunny with gentle breezes during fair weather. But onshore winds generated by coastal storms can change the weather's demeanor rapidly. In general, the coastal climate is much more moderate than that farther inland.

■ **PLANT LIFE**
Fields In late summer, refuge paths lead through fields of yellow goldenrods, black-eyed Susan, purple milkweed, spreading dogbane, and Saint-John's-wort. Feverwort (wild coffee) has paired leaves that resemble milkweed, but the leaves surround the stem; flowers are dull purple-brown and the berries are yellow-orange. Another interesting plant is wild indigo; it has yellow pealike flowers and grows to three feet. The gray-green leaves turn black when dry. The odd whitish upper leaves of the fragrant short-toothed mountain mint will catch your eye, while the buttonlike heads of white flowers remain inconspicuous.

A low-growing plant in sandy soils with aromatic, fernlike foliage and hairy twigs is sweet fern, which is not a fern at all but a shrub. Other shrubs include the familiar bayberry, dwarf oak, common highbush blueberry, and the well-named shiny sumac, the leaves of which appear to have been waxed and polished. Autumn olive, a planted exotic tree, produces fruit and cover for wildlife.
Brackish wetlands The percentage of salt in Trustom Pond waters fluctuates with the tides and rainfall but is always somewhere between the extremes of seawater on the one hand and fresh on the other. Along the pond's shallow, less salty perimeter, you will find wool grass, actually a tall sedge; three-square or chair-

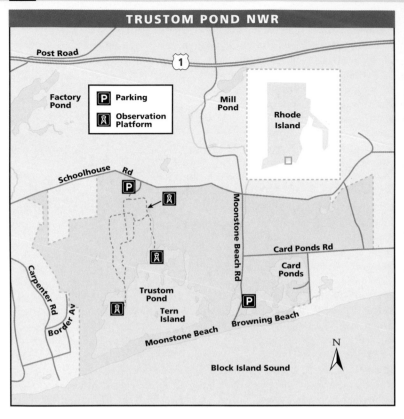

TRUSTOM POND NWR

Post Road

Factory Pond

P Parking

Observation Platform

Mill Pond

Rhode Island

Schoolhouse Rd

Moonstone Beach Rd

Card Ponds Rd

Card Ponds

Carpenter Rd

Border Av

Trustom Pond

Tern Island

Browning Beach

Moonstone Beach

Block Island Sound

N

maker's rush; soft-stem bulrush; freshwater cord grass; cattail; and common reed (at 12 feet tall, the giant among grasses). Aquatic smartweed, which has alternately arranged leaves on a stem up to 6 feet long, is consumed by Trustom Pond's many mute swans.

Freshwater wetlands Wetland indicators are speckled alder, adjacent to the farm pond, and buttonbush, whose roots are waterlogged. Buttonbush displays handsome white globular flower heads about 1.5 inches across. The large oval leaves of bullhead or yellow pond lily float on the farm pond. Moist soils also provide good growing conditions for attractive and fragrant sweet pepperbush. This tall shrub produces spikes of whitish flowers in late summer.

In damp swales near the farm pond, look for pink joe-pye weed, marsh Saint-John's-wort, blue flag iris, and American germander (a mint; note the square stem), whose spike of purplish flowers reaches several feet tall.

Coastal woodland Shrubs, small and medium-sized trees, and vines dominate the landscape. Dominants are black oak and oblong-leaf Juneberry, referred to generically as shad or shadbush. Here poor soils and sculpturing ocean winds combine to produce shad trees of a particularly spreading and picturesque form. They exhibit smooth gray bark, flower in May, and produce fruits favored by birds. The low thicketlike woods also contain numerous black cherry trees and American hazelnut. Straight-branched arrowwood and tartarian honeysuckle, an introduced shrub whose red berries are eaten by robins and other birds, are abundant.

Vines are abundant and conspicuous. Common greenbrier, with rounded heart-shaped leaves and strong spines, is most numerous. Look also for glaucou greenbrier (which has weak spines), wild grape, poison ivy, Virginia creeper (five leaflets that turn bright red in fall), and oriental bittersweet.

The southern tupelo grows near Trustom Pond. This handsome tree produces shiny green leaves (clustered near the twig ends) that turn a brilliant scarlet in fall. Its fruits are blue berries. Examples of southern New England oak-hickory forest are white and pignut hickory and sassafras, which has rough, deeply furrowed bark. Present, too, are red cedar, a pioneering evergreen that invades abandoned pastures; pitch pine; and red maple, which also takes on a spreading form here.

In the partial shade of the shad trees, the large flame-orange flowers of Turk's cap lily hang from stems up to eight feet high, brightening paths in July and August. This photogenic lily has completely re-curved petals, giving rise to its common name. Other trailside flowers include enchanter's nightshade and meadow rue, with small white flowers.

Turk's cap lily

Dunes Saltspray rose, an introduced woody shrub that produces large, pink (sometimes white), fragrant blossoms and very prickly stems, is a familiar shrub along the coast. American beach grass, which blooms in late summer, is the signature dune builder.

■ ANIMAL LIFE

Birds Trustom Pond NWR combines a number of communities—freshwater, saltwater, fields, shrub, and low woodland—to create many ecological niches: the species list numbers about 300. The Atlantic barrier beach hosts two threatened species—least tern and piping plover, a 6-inch-long, sand-colored shorebird. Plovers, which have produced 18 chicks per season most years, return by early April, and the terns arrive a month later; both nest on Moonstone Beach.

Eastern towhee and the three "mimic thrushes" (not thrushes at all)—northern mockingbird, brown thrasher, and gray catbird—prefer thickets. So do house and Carolina wrens and white-eyed vireo (a specialty of essentially southeastern distribution). American kestrel (our smallest falcon); tree swallow, and eastern bluebird, in whose behalf numerous nest boxes have been erected, require open country. Note the wire mesh predator guards attached to box fronts. Tree swallows utilize the boxes as well. In winter 15-inch-long short-eared owls patrol the fields at twilight for voles.

Black-capped chickadee, the related tufted titmouse (the only small gray bird adorned with a crest), white-breasted nuthatch (the "upside down bird"), and cedar waxwing (a crested, tan species), frequent the low woods. Great horned owls, one of the top predators of the refuge, begin nesting in January.

Wetland birds are particularly abundant. Two pairs of fish-eating ospreys nested on the property in 1993, although only one raised young successfully. Ospreys build large nests of sticks in trees or on platforms provided for that purpose.

Listen for the odd song of marsh wrens among the cattails throughout spring and summer. Partial also to freshwater wetlands are the belted kingfisher and the spotted sandpiper, which teeters almost incessantly along shores. You can distinguish the fish crow, a smaller and glossier relative of the American crow, from its larger relative by its higher pitched, more nasal call.

Yellow warbler, a chief host of the brown-headed cowbird (a brood parasite that lays its eggs in the nests of other birds) is common in wet habitats. Along the shores of Trustom Pond, look for elegant snowy egrets (white birds with black bills and legs and bright yellow feet), great blue herons, and green herons. All stalk frogs and fish in the shallows.

A wide assortment of waterfowl, including wood duck (for which big nesting boxes have been erected), American black duck, pied-billed grebe, common moorhen (closely related to coots, but with bright red, yellow-tipped bills), Canada goose, and mute swan frequent the pond.

In addition to the 9-inch-long least tern, the larger common tern is found in the area. The latter nest on offshore rocks and islands, where they are safe from mammalian predators. Many species of shorebirds stop off on their southward migrations in late summer and early fall to rest and feed on the barrier beach and the food-rich shores of Trustom Pond. Ruddy ducks and lesser and greater scaup (greater scaup have more rounded heads with a green sheen) also put in an appearance; some spend the winter, unless the pond freezes over, forcing the birds to move to nearby Ninigret. Double-crested cormorants dive for fish in the pond and "hang their wings out to dry" because they lack oil glands for waterproofing.

Mammals The largest of the 40 species are white-tailed deer, and you may well encounter their tracks. Other, smaller herbivorous species include cottontail rabbit, muskrat, and the rotund woodchuck.

Coyotes, the largest predators, have increased during the past few decades; they feed on rabbits, mice, and voles. Foxes feed on the abundant rodents and fruit in season. River otters frolic in the freshwater wetlands and feast on fish and crayfish. Luxuriantly furred mink prey on bird's eggs, frogs, and most any other animal food. Raccoons, striped skunks, and opossums, all omnivores, consume fruits, insects, rodents, the eggs and young of birds, and carrion. Among the smallest predators are the shrews; the lead gray short-tailed and the tiny brown masked shrew consume insects, worms, and snails. These animals must eat almost constantly and remain under cover much of the time.

Reptiles and amphibians Eastern painted turtles, named for their red undersides, are common in the farm pond where they eat aquatic vegetation, insects, crayfish, snails, and clams; they are most visible when basking. Along the trails in summer, you will find turtle nests that have been dug up by predators (note the

Mute swan

leathery egg shells). The largest farm pond predator is the snapping turtle, which eats almost anything; watch quietly from the observation platform to glimpse its horny beak as it protrudes to breathe.

Common farm-pond amphibians are the bullfrog and green frog. Superficially similar, the smaller green frog bears parallel "pleats" down its back. Their vocalizations, meant to attract females and keep rivals out of their territories, are very different. The deep bass *jug-o-rum* of the bullfrog is familiar to almost everyone; the green frog's vocal effort consists of single or paired guttural notes reminiscent of a plucked banjo string. Young green frogs scream a loud *eek* when startled by a predator or passerby.

Fishes Just offshore are sculpin, a bizarre-looking groundfish with fanlike pectoral fins; little skate (a 2-foot-long shark relative); and flounder, a pancake-shaped bottom feeder that is able to modify its coloration so as to blend in with the ocean floor.

Invertebrates Transom Pond is a great place to observe insects and butterflies. The big yellow-and-black tiger swallowtail and the lovely red-spotted purple (the red spots on this butterfly are on the underwings) are among the most attractive. Early in summer, watch for red admiral and painted lady in the fields. There are also common wood nymph, a moderately large brown butterfly with large blue and yellow "eye spots," and the familiar monarch, a long-distance migrant that appears in large numbers along the coast in late summer and early fall. The most spectacular day-flying moth is the yellow-and-maroon hummingbird hawkmoth, which hovers and extracts sweet nectar from tubular flowers.

Rocks encrusted with barnacles in Trustom Pond indicate that storms drive saltwater into the usually freshwater body. Northern lobster, common oyster, sea clam (all economically important species), Forbes' asterias (a sea star), and green sea urchin were among the many bottom-dwelling saltwater invertebrates that fell victim to the 1996 oil spill.

ACTIVITIES

■ **SWIMMING AND CAMPING:** Moonstone Beach (South Kingstown Town Beach) is popular. Other excellent sandy beaches nearby are East Matunuck and Green Hill.

Camping is not permitted on refuge property; the nearest public campground is Burlington Camping Area, off Rte. 1, near Ninigret NWR.

■ **WILDLIFE OBSERVATION:** To enhance your enjoyment of Trustom Pond's large diversity of wildlife, take advantage of the refuge's observation platforms and well-maintained trails. Two platforms overlook Trustom Pond, from which you can spot waterfowl (the best pond view is from the western platform).

EXOTIC MUTE SWANS Some 150 exotic mute swans dwell on Trustom Pond and its shores, causing a tremendous impact on the nutrient balance of the pond. The excrement from so many of these large birds results in a great amount of nutrient loading. The resultant algal blooms rob the water of much of its oxygen as the algae decay, a process that has quite a negative impact on the fish and other aquatic wildlife in the pond—as well as the predators, both bird and mammal, that feed upon them. The refuge staff is working to minimize the impact of these exotic birds.

Watch nesting ospreys from platforms or trails and check out the observation decks along the shore of the farm pond, which pulsates with amphibian life. A bird-feeding station is also located here.

In April and May, chubby long-billed male American woodcocks perform their dazzling courtship flights in fields near the water. Hawks migrating southward along the coast reach peak numbers from mid-September to early October, while significant numbers of migrant and wintering ducks choose the protected waters of Trustom Pond for feeding and resting.

■ **PHOTOGRAPHY:** There is much to photograph—from the gorgeous Turk's cap lily to colorful butterflies, nesting ospreys, and basking painted turtles. Are all readily accessible from trails and observation platforms, which also provide excellent panoramas of Trustom Pond.

■ **HIKES AND WALKS:** About three miles of wide, gently sloping, wood-chipped trails traverse the property (fine gravel and short-grass surfaces on some); all lead to Trustom Pond. The trails, like other refuge facilities, are well maintained and a joy to use. A sanitary chemical toilet is at the parking area. The observation platforms are wonderful places to have a snack and enjoy the views. You may well want to take more than three hours (the parking limit) to explore this attractive property.

■ **PUBLICATIONS:** "Wildlife Refuges of Rhode Island" and "Birds of the National Wildlife Refuges of Rhode Island" are U.S. Fish & Wildlife Service brochures available from the Ninigret NWR office.

Missisquoi NWR
Swanton, Vermont

Ferns and hardwoods, Missisquoi NWR

The most extensive freshwater marshland in Vermont is a haven for plants and animals who prefer life in the wet. Vociferous red-and-yellow-epauletted red-winged blackbird males voice creaky refrains from cattail stalks, and marsh wrens sing their songs long after nightfall. Floodplain forests of elm and silver maple thrive in river-deposited mud, while lush wild rice crowds the shoreline. Even the views are best enjoyed from the water: A shimmery Lake Champlain and the bluish mountains beyond look especially idyllic from a boat launched into the Missisquoi River.

HISTORY

The first European to lay eyes on Lake Champlain (and the land that is now the refuge) was the French explorer Samuel de Champlain, in 1609. From a large, important Abenaki village (named *Missisquoi*, Abenaki for "place of flint"), in the vicinity of what is now the refuge, the war chief Grey Lock raided Colonial settlements during the 1720s. The lake also played a prominent role in the French and Indian War, the American Revolution, and the War of 1812. The 6,338-acre refuge was established in 1943 as an important feeding, resting, and breeding area for migratory birds, especially waterfowl.

GETTING THERE

From Burlington, travel north on I-89 about 45 mi. to Swanton. Take Exit 21 (Rte. 78) and drive west, then north for 2 mi. past the town of Swanton, to the refuge headquarters on the left.

■ **SEASON:** Refuge open year-round.
■ **HOURS:** Refuge open dawn to dusk; office: Mon.–Fri., 8 a.m.–4:30 p.m.
■ **FEES:** Admission to the refuge is free.
■ **ADDRESS:** Missisquoi NWR, P.O. Box 163, Swanton, VT 05488-0163.

■ **TELEPHONE, FAX, AND E-MAIL:** Refuge Headquarters: 802/868-4781; fax: 802/868-2379; e-mail: R5RW_MSQNWR@fws.gov

TOURING MISSISQUOI

■ **BY AUTOMOBILE:** You may drive through the middle of the refuge on Rte. 78. Vehicles may not be left on the refuge overnight.

■ **BY FOOT:** One trail, about 1.5 miles long, originates at the headquarters parking area on the property's southern end, where a chemical toilet accessible to the disabled is available. You can also walk along Mac's Bend Rd. that borders the Missisquoi River for about 1 mile. Refuge trails are also open for cross-country skiing.

■ **BY BICYCLE:** Ride from Swanton or the refuge headquarters through the middle of the refuge on Rte. 78 and then onto Shore Rd. and Tabor Rd. (off the refuge), in roughly a rectangle, then back to Rte. 78 for the return to the Visitor Center. A short but pleasant ride down Mac's Bend Rd. follows the scenic Missisquoi River. Round-trip distance from Visitor Center, including Mac's Bend Rd. spur, is about 17 miles.

■ **BY CANOE, KAYAK, OR BOAT:** The best way to experience Missisquoi is by water. Boating is permitted along the Missisquoi River and on Lake Champlain, and watercraft may be launched into the river from two public ramps on Mac's Bend Rd. The first (First, or Louie's, Landing) is about 0.75 mile beyond the headquarters on the right, near the junction of Rte. 78 and Mac's Bend Rd., and is open all year. The second (open from Sept. 1 to the end of the waterfowl hunting season in Dec.) is about 1 mile beyond the first. Toilets and benches are at the boat launch sites.

Other points where boats may be launched include a public ramp on the shore of Lake Champlain, just north of Rte. 78, off the refuge, near the Missisquoi Bay Bridge, and another about 3 miles south of Rte. 78. Take Tabor Rd. left, follow it to the junction with Shore Rd., turn left and follow Shore Rd. for a short distance before turning right and following it to the lakeshore.

Canoes and motorboats can be rented and launched at the private Campbell Bay Campground at Donaldson Point, adjacent to the refuge; take Rte. 78 west to Campbell Rd. on the right. Negotiating offshore lake waters in a canoe from this point can be tricky.

Portions of the refuge, closed to boaters to protect wildlife habitat, are posted with "Area Closed" signs.

WHAT TO SEE

■ **LANDSCAPE AND CLIMATE** The refuge, occupying part of a peninsula that extends into the northern part of Lake Champlain, touches the Canadian border and encompasses river delta, floodplain forest, marshes, and fields. Nearly the entire Missisquoi River delta, an area rich in wildlife, lies within the refuge; here the river, which originates in the Green Mountains to the east, empties into Missisquoi Bay. The vast Missisquoi delta marshes are only a few feet above the level of the lake and are inundated each spring.

Black Creek and Maquam Creek are slow, meandering streams, covered in places by a floating mat of duckweed. Red maple dominates the bottomland forest. The two creeks, whose waters are the color of root beer, converge at Lookout Point, a scenic spot where waterfowl and other wildlife may be viewed to good advantage.

All this water makes for high atmospheric moisture, especially in summer

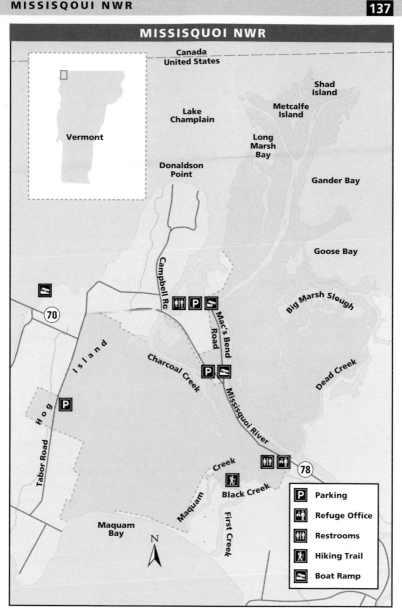

MISSISQUOI NWR

Canada
United States

Shad
Island

Metcalfe
Island

Lake
Champlain

Vermont

Long
Marsh
Bay

Donaldson
Point

Gander Bay

Goose Bay

Campbell Rd

Big Marsh Slough

70

Mac's Bend Road

Charcoal Creek

Dead Creek

Island

Missisquoi River

Hog

Tabor Road

Creek

78

Maquam
Bay

Maquam

Black Creek

First Creek

| P | Parking |
| Refuge Office |
| Restrooms |
| Hiking Trail |
| Boat Ramp |

N

Water vapor is shed as it rides up nearby mountains, and thunderstorms often build rather quickly on summer afternoons. The sun can be hot, and the humidity adds to the potential for discomfort; breezes off the big lake, however, usually have a cooling effect. Lake Champlain generally does not freeze over completely (this area has the state's mildest climate), but it did so in 1904 and 1994. Ice recedes from the lake from mid-March to late April, depending on the season.

■ **PLANT LIFE**
Floodplain (riverine) forest Despite their northern location (at the 45th parallel), Missisquoi forests more resemble southern New England woodlands:

Low elevation and abundant moisture combine to nurture this classic bottom-land forest. Thickly timbered riverbanks are lined with overarching silver maples, while red maples dominate Black Creek. Another giant along the watercourses is the rough-barked eastern cottonwood. The flaky gray trunks of swamp white oak are wrapped with wire netting to keep beavers at bay. Organic matter deposited by floodwaters creates ideal growing conditions; willows root in the mud of the river delta, and silky dogwood bordering the creeks forms a dense growth. The feathery fronds of ferns can be seen on slightly higher ground.

White-blossomed aromatic water lilies float on calm backwaters. Another plant with floating leaves is water shield. Much smaller are watermeal and duckweed,which, in the thousands, form a solid mat on the surface of Black Creek; both are important duck food. You may also encounter mats of light-green filamentous *Spirogyra* alga on the creek's surface. Bubbles of oxygen, a by-product of photosynthesis, add to the surface's slimy appearance.

River delta marshes The fertile Missisquoi River delta shelters dense growths of wild rice, freshwater cord grass, cattails, and soft-stem bulrush, all of which yield a bounty for waterfowl and other wildlife. Wild rice, which can rise 10 feet tall, is a delicacy for humans, too. It has wide leaves, a tuft of female "flowers" at the top of the stem, and drooping straw-to-purplish-colored male flowers below.

An especially vigorous growth of emergent plants, near the shore, includes broad-leaved arrowhead, which has big triangular leaves and white three-petaled flowers, and pickerelweed, which puts out a purple flower stalk in midsummer. In shallow water you will also find bur reed (whose seed heads look like medieval spiked clubs), water plantain (actually an arrowhead), and water hemlock (reputed to have felled Socrates); its flower heads resemble those of the related Queen Anne's lace.

Common goldeneye

From a boat, watch for the submerged ribbonlike leaves of water celery fluttering in the current. Eurasian water milfoil, an exotic that can outproduce native plants and fill a water body so completely that it becomes inhospitable for fish and other creatures, also makes navigation nearly impossible at the delta mouth. Because cuttings of the plant quickly regenerate (the leaves look like weatherbeaten feathers), it is easily transferred from one body to another on boat propellers. Excess nutrients from faulty septic systems and residential and agricultural runoff exacerbate the problem.

Besides the natural marshlands, the refuge includes 1,800 acres of managed wetlands formed by three impoundments. These pools are a mix of open water and rich stands of emergent plants, shrubs, and wooded swamps that offer food and cover for ducks and geese.

Upland forest Dry ground is hard to come by here, and red oak, a valuable timber tree, prefers well-drained sites. Woodland wildflowers generally bloom in spring, before the sun's rays are deflected by the canopy. In May, Canada mayflower, with its dainty white flowers, carpets the forest floor, especially under pines. Other spring bloomers include partridgeberry, a creeping plant with small, paired dark-green leaves and white flowers; large-flowered bellwort (a yellow drooping flower); and jack-in-the-pulpit. In summer, look for the woodland sunflower along the forest edge. In late summer, the purplish, pealike flowers of groundnut open and climb over shrubs; it has an edible tuber.

■ ANIMAL LIFE

Birds Missisquoi offers birders more than 200 species. In the summer, scan for the little pied-billed grebe or hell-diver in marshy ponds and along the river delta. The crow-sized green heron, the somewhat larger black-crowned night heron, the camouflaged and reclusive American bittern, and the stately great blue heron wade through the shallows, looking for telltale movements from their prey. One of the largest great blue heron rookeries in Vermont is on Shad Island in the delta.

Nesting are American black duck (note the bright white wing linings in flight), little blue-winged teal, the exquisite wood duck, hooded merganser (a fish- and invertebrate-eater), and common goldeneye. Male goldeneyes display iridescent green heads marked by a white cheek spot. The latter three are all cavity nesters.

Nearly 200 nesting structures have been placed throughout the refuge for their use.

Listen for the elusive Virginia rail, who reveals its presence by its odd grunting and whinnying vocalizations, usually at dawn and dusk. The expression "skinny as a rail" refers to these marsh dwellers, who generally prefer to walk than fly. Watch for common moorhen, a cootlike bird with a bright red bill. Belted kingfishers (the female has two "belts," one blue and the other chestnut) often go unnoticed until you hear the rattling flight call or see it

Osprey with captured meal

plunge-diving for fish. Another fish-eater is the magnificent osprey. Ospreys build sprawling stick nests in trees and atop platforms, often on islands where they seek safety from predators. With their talons they pluck dead branches in flight for nest construction.

More likely to be seen swimming and diving for fish on Missisquoi Bay is the blackish double-crested cormorant, a member of the pelican family. Another species often found at the seashore are the graceful terns. Smaller and more delicate than gulls, with pointed wings and sharp beaks, these fish-eaters also nest on islands in the lake. Two species to watch for are common tern and the smaller black tern, a marsh nester unusual in New England. The common tern is listed as endangered in Vermont.

Mixed woodland and wetland communities host eye-catching rose-breasted grosbeaks, wood warblers, and olive-drab vireos and flycatchers. Open fields and meadows are home to the American kestrel, primarily an insect eater. This lovely falcon is our smallest nesting raptor. Kestrels usually select abandoned flicker holes but will also use nest boxes.

Mammals Among 34 species identified, white-tailed deer, muskrat, and raccoon are among the most frequently seen. Raccoons thrive in bottomland forests where large trees with hollows provide den sites and watery habitats provide plenty of food—frogs, crayfish, and waterfowl eggs and young.

Beaver bank lodges, runs (pathways from woods to water), and felled trees are common sights. An impressive lodge is visible along the Missisquoi River. You may also find territorial scent posts—small piles of mud upon which these rodents have secreted castoreum, with its a distinctive musky odor. Strict vegetarians, beavers tend to be active early and late, whereas muskrats are often abroad by day. The latter construct lodges of cattails and mud, upon which ducks and geese often place their nests. River otters also use abandoned beaver and muskrat lodges. Look for their scats, often composed solely of fish scales, along the trail. Sleek mink, the otter's smaller relative, are also present.

Oak woodlands produce mast (nuts, seeds, and acorns) that squirrels find delectable; squirrels in turn provide nourishment for predators like the fisher. The big weasel is an occasional visitor. New England cottontails and snowshoe hares inhabit upland woods. Snowshoe hares are famous for their enormous hind feet. Both are prey for the occasional visiting bobcat or coyote.

Reptiles and amphibians One of the most interesting of the refuge's reptiles is the map turtle, which prefers large rivers and lakes; it dwells both in Lake Champlain and in the Missisquoi River, where basking on a log is a favorite pastime and the foods of choice are snails and crayfish. Young turtles have an intricate

Eastern spiny softshell turtle

maplike pattern on their backs, and their heads and necks are marked with a complex pattern of yellow swirls. Eastern spiny softshells, unusual turtles with flat, leathery, flexible shells, are powerful swimmers and can move rapidly on land as well. Both turtles occur nowhere else in the region.

Because it frequently swims on the surface, the northern water snake, a harmless species, may be mistaken for the poisonous water moccasin. The water snake preys on small fish and frogs.

Brown spotted leopard frogs are abundant in late summer along the Black Creek Trail. Other species are common as well, including corpulent bullfrogs that reside in the sluggish waters of the delta. Here, males vigorously defend feeding territories from rivals.

Fishes This watery world harbors a wonderful array of fish, including codlike

MISSISQUOI HUNTING AND FISHING SEASONS

Hunting
(Seasons may vary)

	Jan	Feb	Mar	Apr	May	Jun	Jul	Aug	Sep	Oct	Nov	Dec
white-tailed deer (using following hunting methods)												
bow										X		X
firearm											X	
muzzle loader												X
gray squirrel									X	X	X	X
cottontail rabbit	X	X	X						X	X	X	X
snowshoe hare	X	X	X						X	X	X	X
ruffed grouse									X	X	X	X
American crow			X	X				X	X	X		
bobcat	X	X									X	X
red and gray fox	X	X	X	X	X	X	X	X	X	X	X	X
coyote	X	X	X	X	X	X	X	X	X	X	X	X
raccoon	X	X								X	X	X
muskrat			X	X								
wild turkey (using following hunting methods)												
bow or firearm					X							
bow only					X					X	X	

Fishing

	Jan	Feb	Mar	Apr	May	Jun	Jul	Aug	Sep	Oct	Nov	Dec
landlocked salmon				X	X	X	X	X				
trout				X	X	X	X	X	X			
walleye	X	X	X		X	X	X	X	X	X	X	X
largemouth and smallmouth bass (using following fishing methods)												
catch						X	X	X	X	X	X	
catch and release				X	X	X						
chain pickerel	X	X	X	X	X	X	X	X	X	X	X	X
northern pike	X	X	X	X	X	X	X	X	X	X	X	X
muskellunge	X	X	X	X	X	X	X	X	X	X	X	X
yellow perch	X	X	X	X	X	X	X	X	X	X	X	X

Frog picking is permitted from July 15 to Sept. 30 in mowed refuge fields along Rte. 78 and Mac's Bend Rd.; limit is 12 frogs per person per day. A valid state hunting license or a combination hunting/fishing license is required.

For information on current fishing regulations for Lake Champlain (which may vary), license requirements, seasons, and bag limits, consult refuge office.

Portions of the refuge are open to waterfowl, deer, and small-game hunting in accordance with state and federal regulations. Hunters and anglers are asked to stay at least 75 feet from nesting structures to avoid disturbing wildlife. Current regulations are available from the refuge office. For current digest of state fish and game laws, write Vermont Fish & Wildlife, 103 S. Main St., Waterbury, VT 05670, 002/244-7331.

burbot; bowfin (distinguished by its one long dorsal fin), longnose gar, an unusual fish bearing thick diamond-shaped scales; and landlocked Atlantic salmon. Salmon frequent the Missisquoi River in spring and fall.

The most sought-after game fish in the delta are walleye—a relative of the yellow perch—and northern pike. Pike frequent coves and backwaters with aquatic vegetation.

Invertebrates Globular jellylike bryozoan colonies as big as volleyballs float on the surface of Maquam Creek. Attached to submerged tree branches, these assemblages of primitive single-celled organisms feed on microscopic creatures; food particles are directed toward each animal's mouth by hairlike cilia. Freshwater clams siphon and strain food particles from the Missisquoi and are relished by raccoons and otters.

When walking on paths through shrub wetlands in summer and fall, look for bits of white cottony lint on alder twigs. Look closer, and you will see the "lint" actually move! These are woolly alder aphids. The wool is a waxy material exuded by the insect as it feeds on the shrub's sap.

Predatory dragonflies and damselflies are some of the most active—and therefore among the most conspicuous—insects in the wetlands. The large green darner keeps the mosquito population in check. Another common species is the red skimmer. In the summer, newly emerged aggregations of thousands of whirligig beetles gyrate about on the surface of slow-moving creeks, using the echoes from their own ripples to help find insects.

ACTIVITIES

■ **SWIMMING AND CAMPING:** There are no suitable swimming locations on the refuge. Camping is not permitted on refuge property; private campgrounds are at nearby Campbell Bay Campground (open May-Sept.) and at a private campground south of the refuge, off Rte. 78, in Swanton.

■ **WILDLIFE OBSERVATION:** Walk Black Creek and Maquam Creek trails for a blend of woodland and wetland wildlife. Lookout Point, where the creeks merge, is a scenic vantage point from which to see waterfowl. Beaver lodges are here and at the beginning of the Maquam Trail. Observe wildlife also from Mac's Bend Rd., which parallels the Missisquoi River.

To really appreciate the refuge and its wildlife, put a canoe into the Missisquoi River and paddle out to the delta and Lake Champlain to find waterfowl, beavers, muskrats, turtles, herons, and other wildlife. The refuge hosts 20,000 waterfowl during autumn migration.

■ **PHOTOGRAPHY:** It would be tough to beat the panoramic views of Lake Champlain from the Missisquoi River delta on a summer or fall day. Bluish mountains are visible on the northeastern horizon across Missisquoi Bay. Cruise slowly down the river to photograph lush riverbank vegetation and the wildlife it harbors.

The two creek trails, especially Maquam Creek, afford ample opportunities for close-ups of ferns or long shots of wood ducks, herons, and dragonflies. Lookout Point is also picturesque. Lighting situations can and do run the gamut from deep shade to bright sun, especially on the water.

■ **HIKES AND WALKS:** Maquam Creek and Black Creek trails represent the only foot access to the refuge except for Mac's Bend Rd. A leaflet on the trails is available. The trails are usually very wet from April through June, when shin-high boots are recommended. Insect repellent may be necessary during summer.

■ **SEASONAL EVENTS:** For an events schedule, contact refuge headquarters.

■ **PUBLICATIONS:** Five leaflets are available from refuge headquarters and at the Black Creek and Maquam Creek Trailhead: "Missisquoi National Wildlife Refuge," "Black Creek and Maquam Creek Trail—A Walk in a Wetland Habitat," "Birds—Missisquoi NWR," "Mammals—Missisquoi NWR," and "Fishing on the Missisquoi Delta—Missisquoi NWR."

Appendix

NONVISITABLE NATIONAL WILDLIFE REFUGES

Below is a list of other National Wildlife Refuges in the New England states. These refuges are not open to the public.

Seal Island NWR
c/o Petit Manan NWR
P.O. Box 279
Milbridge, ME 04658
207/546-2124
A nesting ground for the Atlantic puffin, successfully reintroduced here after a 100-year absence.

Mashpee NWR
c/o Great Meadows NWR
Weir Hill Road
Sudbury, MA 01776
978/443-4661

Massasoit NWR
c/o Great Meadows NWR
Weir Hill Road
Sudbury, MA 01776
978/443-4661
A research and habitat area for the endangered Plymouth red-bellied turtle.

Nomans Land Island NWR
c/o Great Meadows NWR
Weir Hill Road
Sudbury, MA 01776
978/443-4661
A major staging area for peregrine falcons.

Thacher Island NWR
c/o Parker River NWR
261 Northern Boulevard
Plum Island
Newburyport, MA 01950
978/465-5753

Pettaquamscutt Cove NWR
c/o Ninigret NWR
P.O. Box 307
Charlestown, RI 02813
401/364-9124

FEDERAL RECREATION FEES

Some—but not all—NWRs and other federal outdoor recreation areas require payment of entrance or use fees (the latter for facilities such as boat ramps). There are several congressionally authorized entrance fee passes:

■ **ANNUAL PASSES**

Golden Eagle Passport Valid for most national parks, monuments, historic sites, recreation areas, and national wildlife refuges. Admits the passport signee and any accompanying passengers in a private vehicle. Good for 12 months. Purchase at any federal area where an entrance fee is charged. The 1999 fee for this pass was $50.

Federal Duck Stamp Authorized in 1934 as a federal permit to hunt waterfowl and as a source of revenue to purchase wetlands, the Duck Stamp now also serves as an annual entrance pass to NWRs. Admits holder and accompanying passengers in a private vehicle. Good from July 1 for one year. Valid for entrance fees only. Purchase at post offices and many NWRs or from Federal Duck Stamp Office, 800/782-6724, or at Wal-Mart, Kmart, or other sporting-goods stores.

■ **LIFETIME PASSES**

Golden Access Passport Lifetime entrance pass—for persons who are blind or permanently disabled to most national parks and NWRs. Admits signee and any accompanying passengers in a private vehicle. Provides 50 percent discount on federal-use fees charged for facilities and services such as camping or boating. Must be obtained in person at a federal recreation area charging a fee. Obtain by showing proof of medically determined permanent disability or eligibility for receiving benefits under federal law.

Golden Age Passport Lifetime entrance pass—for persons 62 years of age or older—to national parks and NWRs. Admits signee and any accompanying passengers in a private vehicle. Provides 50 percent discount on federal use fees charged for facilities and services such as camping or boating. Must be obtained in person at a federal recreation area charging a fee. One-time $10 processing charge. Available only to U.S. citizens or permanent residents.

For more information, contact your local federal recreation area for a copy of the "Federal Recreation Passport Program" brochure.

VOLUNTEER ACTIVITIES

Each year, 30,000 Americans volunteer their time and talents to help the U.S. Fish & Wildlife Service conserve the nation's precious wildlife and their habitats. Volunteers conduct Fish & Wildlife population surveys, lead public tours and other recreational programs, protect endangered species, restore habitat, and run environmental education programs.

The NWR volunteer program is as diverse as the refuges themselves. There is no "typical" Fish & Wildlife Service volunteer. The different ages, backgrounds, and experiences volunteers bring with them are among the greatest strengths of the program. Refuge managers also work with their neighbors, conservation groups, colleges and universities, and business organizations.

A growing number of people are taking pride in the stewardship of local National Wildlife Refuges by organizing nonprofit organizations to support individual refuges. These refuge community partner groups, which numbered about 200 in the year 2000, have been so helpful that the Fish & Wildlife Service, National Audubon Society, National Wildlife Refuge Association, and National Fish & Wildlife Foundation now carry out a national program called the "Refuge System Friends Initiative" to coordinate and strengthen existing partnerships, to jump-start new ones, and to organize other efforts promoting community involvement in activities associated with the National Wildlife Refuge System.

For more information on how to get involved, visit the Fish & Wildlife Service Homepage at http://www.refuges.fws.gov; or contact one of the Volunteer Coordinator offices listed on the U.S. Fish & Wildlife General Information list of addresses below or the U. S. Fish & Wildlife Service, Division of Refuges, Attn: Volunteer Coordinator, 4401 N. Fairfax Dr., Arlington, VA 22203; 703/358-2303.

U.S. FISH & WILDLIFE GENERAL INFORMATION

Below is a list of addresses to contact for more information concerning the National Wildlife Refuge System.

U.S. Fish & Wildlife Service Division of Refuges
4401 N. Fairfax Dr., Room 670
Arlington, Virginia 22203
703/358-1744

F&W Service Publications:
800/344-WILD

U.S. Fish & Wildlife Service Pacific Region
911 NE 11th Ave.
Eastside Federal Complex
Portland, OR 97232-4181
External Affairs Office: 503/231-6120
Volunteer Coordinator: 503/231-2077
The Pacific Region office oversees the refuges in California, Hawaii, Idaho, Nevada, Oregon, and Washington.

U.S. Fish & Wildlife Service Southwest Region
500 Gold Ave., SW
P.O. Box 1306
Albuquerque, NM 87103
External Affairs Office: 505/248-6285
Volunteer Coordinator: 505/248-6635
The Southwest Region office oversees the refuges in Arizona, New Mexico, Oklahoma, and Texas.

U.S. Fish & Wildlife Service Great Lakes–Big Rivers Region
1 Federal Dr.
Federal Building
Fort Snelling, MN 55111-4056
External Affairs Office: 612/713-5310
Volunteer Coordinator: 612/713-5444
The Great Lakes–Big Rivers Region office oversees the refuges in Iowa, Illinois, Indiana, Michigan, Minnesota, Missouri, Ohio, and Wisconsin.

U.S. Fish & Wildlife Service Southeast Region
1875 Century Center Blvd.
Atlanta, GA 30345
External Affairs Office: 404/679-7288
Volunteer Coordinator: 404/679-7178
The Southeast Region office oversees the refuges in Alabama, Arkansas, Florida, Georgia, Kentucky, Louisiana, Mississippi, North Carolina, South Carolina, Tennessee, and Puerto Rico.

U.S. Fish & Wildlife Service Northeast Region
300 Westgate Center Dr.
Hadley, MA 01035-9589
External Affairs Office: 413/253-8325
Volunteer Coordinator: 413/253-8303
The Northeast Region office oversees the refuges in Connecticut, Delaware, Massachusetts, Maine, New Hampshire, New Jersey, New York, Pennsylvania, Rhode Island, Vermont, Virginia, and West Virginia.

U.S. Fish & Wildlife Service Mountain–Prairie Region
Denver Federal Center
P. O. Box 25486
Denver, CO 80225
External Affairs Office: 303/236-7905
Volunteer Coordinator: 303/236-8145, x 614
The Mountain–Prairie Region office oversees the refuges in Colorado, Kansas, Montana, Nebraska, North Dakota, South Dakota, Utah, and Wyoming.

U.S. Fish & Wildlife Service Alaska Region
1011 East Tudor Rd.
Anchorage, AK 99503
External Affairs Office: 907/786-3309

NATIONAL AUDUBON SOCIETY WILDLIFE SANCTUARIES

National Audubon Society's 100 sanctuaries comprise 150,000 acres and include a wide range of habitats. Audubon managers and scientists use the sanctuaries for rigorous field research and for testing wildlife management strategies. The following is an alphabetical list of 24 sanctuaries open to the public, with contact address and numbers. Sanctuaries open by appointment only are marked with an asterisk.

EDWARD M. BRIGHAM III ALKALI LAKE SANCTUARY*
c/o North Dakota State Office
118 Broadway, Suite 502
Fargo, ND 58102
701/298-3373

FRANCIS BEIDLER FOREST SANCTUARY
336 Sanctuary Rd.
Harleyville, SC 29448
843/462-2160

BORESTONE MOUNTAIN SANCTUARY
P.O. Box 524
118 Union Square
Dover-Foxcroft, ME 04426
207/564-7946

CLYDE E. BUCKLEY SANCTUARY
1305 Germany Rd.
Frankfort, KY 40601
606/873-5711

BUTTERCUP WILDLIFE SANCTUARY*
c/o New York State Office
200 Trillium Lane
Albany, NY 12203
518/869-9731

CONSTITUTION MARSH SANCTUARY
P.O. Box 174
Cold Spring, NY, 10516
914/265-2601

CORKSCREW SWAMP SANCTUARY
375 Sanctuary Rd. West
Naples, FL 34120
941/348-9151

FLORIDA COASTAL ISLANDS SANCTUARY*
410 Ware Blvd., Suite 702
Tampa, FL 33619
813/623-6826

EDWARD L. & CHARLES E. GILLMOR SANCTUARY*
3868 Marsha Dr.
West Valley City, UT 84120
801/966-0464

KISSIMMEE PRAIRIE SANCTUARY*
100 Riverwoods Circle
Lorida, FL 33857
941/467-8497

MAINE COASTAL ISLANDS SANCTUARIES*
Summer (June–Aug.):
12 Audubon Rd.
Bremen, ME 04551
207/529-5828

MILES WILDLIFE SANCTUARY*
99 West Cornwall Rd.
Sharon, CT 06069
860/364-0048

NORTH CAROLINA COASTAL ISLANDS SANCTUARY*
720 Market St.
Wilmington, NC 28401-4647
910/762-9534

NORTHERN CALIFORNIA SANCTUARIES*
c/o California State Office
555 Audubon Place
Sacramento, CA 95825
916/481-5440

PINE ISLAND SANCTUARY*
P.O. Box 174
Poplar Branch, NC 27965
919/453-2838

RAINEY WILDLIFE SANCTUARY*
10149 Richard Rd.
Abbeville, LA 70510-9216
318/898-5969 (Beeper: leave message)

RESEARCH RANCH SANCTUARY*
HC1, Box 44
Elgin, AZ 85611
520/455-5522

RHEINSTROM HILL WILDLIFE SANCTUARY*
P.O. Box 1
Craryville, NY 12521
518/325-5203

THEODORE ROOSEVELT SANCTUARY
134 Cove Rd.
Oyster Bay, NY 11771
516/922-3200

LILLIAN ANNETTE ROWE SANCTUARY
44450 Elm Island Rd.
Gibbon, NE 68840
308/468-5282

SABAL PALM GROVE SANCTUARY
P.O. Box 5052
Brownsville, TX 78523
956/541-8034

SILVER BLUFF SANCTUARY*
4542 Silver Bluff Rd.
Jackson, SC 29831
803/827-0781

STARR RANCH SANCTUARY*
100 Bell Canyon Rd.
Trabuco Canyon, CA 92678
949/858-0309

TEXAS COASTAL ISLANDS SANCTUARIES
c/o Texas State Office
2525 Wallingwood, Suite 301
Austin, TX 78746
512/306-0225

BIBLIOGRAPHY & RESOURCES

Aquatic biology
Morgan, Ann Haven. *Field Book of Ponds and Streams: An Introduction to the Life of Fresh Water*, New York: G. P. Putnam's Sons, 1930.

Audio recordings
Peterson, Roger Tory. *Field Guide to Bird Songs—Eastern/Central North America*, Boston: Houghton Mifflin, 1999.

Voices of the Night: The Calls of the Frogs & Toads of Eastern North America, Ithaca, N.Y.: Cornell Laboratory of Ornithology, 1982.

Walton, Richard K. and Robert W. Lawson. *Birding by Ear: Guide to Bird Song Identification* (1989) and *More Birding by Ear: Eastern and Central* (1994), Boston: Houghton Mifflin.

Behavior guides
Stokes Nature Guides titles include: *A Guide to Nature in Winter* (1979), *A Guide to Bird Behavior* (vol. 1, 1983; vol. 2, 1985; vol. 3, 1989), *A Guide to Animal Tracking and Behavior* (1998), *A Guide to Observing Insect Lives* (1983), all by Donald W. Stokes; and *A Guide to Amphibians and Reptiles* (1990), by Thomas F. Tyning, Boston: Little, Brown.

Birds
Walton, Richard K. *Bird Finding in New England*, Colorado Springs: American Birding Association, 1988.

Fry, Adam J. *Bird Walks in Rhode Island, Exploring the Ocean State's Best Sanctuaries*, Woodstock, Vt.: Backcountry Publications, 1992.

Bird Observer. *A Birder's Guide to Eastern Massachusetts*, Colorado Springs: American Birding Association, 1994.

Pierson, Elizabeth C., Jan Erik Pierson, and Peter D. Vickery. *A Birder's Guide to Maine*, Camden, Maine: Down East Books, 1996.

Delorey, Alan. *A Birder's Guide to New Hampshire*, Colorado Springs: American Birding Association, 1996.

Ehrlich, Paul R., David S. Dobkin, and Darryl Wheye. *The Birder's Handbook, A Field Guide to the Natural History of North American Birds*, New York: Simon & Schuster, 1988.

Veit, Richard and Wayne R. Petersen. *Birds of Massachusetts*, Lincoln, Mass.: Massachusetts Audubon Society, 1993.

Devine, Arnold "Buzz" and Dwight G. Smith. *Connecticut Birding Guide*, Dexter, Mich.: Thomson-Shore. 1996.

Botany
Brown, Lauren. *Grasses, An Identification Guide*, Boston: Houghton Mifflin, 1979.

Magee, Dennis W. *Freshwater Wetlands, A Guide to Common Indicator Plants of the Northeast*, Amherst: University of Massachusetts Press, 1981.

Newcomb, Lawrence. *Newcomb's Wildflower Guide*, Boston: Little, Brown 1977.

Sutton, Ann and Myron. *National Audubon Society Nature Guides, Eastern Forests*, New York: Alfred A. Knopf, 1985.

Wiggers, Raymond. *The Plant Explorer's Guide to New England*, Missoula, Mont.: Mountain Press Publishing, 1994.

Cultural history
Allport, Susan. *Sermons in Stone*, New York: W. W. Norton, 1990.

Cronon, William. *Changes in the Land: Indians, Colonists, and the Ecology of New England*, New York: Hill and Wang, 1983.

Russell, Howard S. *Indian New England Before the Mayflower*, Hanover, N.H.: University Press of New England, 1985.

Field guides

Griggs, Jack. *American Bird Conservancy's Field Guide, All the Birds of North America*, New York: Harper Perennial, 1997.

Field Guide to the Birds of North America, 3rd Edition, Washington, D.C.: National Geographic Society, 1999.

Peterson Field Guides, Boston: Houghton Mifflin.: *Atlantic Seashore*, by Kenneth L. Gosner (1978); *Eastern and Central Reptiles and Amphibians*, by Roger Conant (1975); *Eastern Birds*, by Roger Tory Peterson (1980); *Eastern Butterflies*, by Paul A. Opler and Vichai Malikul (1992); *Eastern Forests*, by John C. Kricher (1988); *Ferns*, Boughton Cobb (1963); *Trees and Shrubs*, by George A. Petrides (1972); *Wildflowers*, by Roger Tory Peterson and Margaret McKenny (1968).

Geology

Thomson, Betty Flanders. *The Changing Face of New England*, Boston: Houghton Mifflin, 1977.

Bell, Michael. *The Face of Connecticut, People, Geology, and the Land*, Hartford: State Geological and Natural History Survey of Connecticut, 1985.

Sorrell, Charles A. *A Guide to Field Identification, Rocks and Minerals*, New York: Golden Press, 1973.

Jorgenson, Neil. *A Guide to New England's Landscape*, Chester, Conn.: Globe Pequot Press, 1977.

Pellant, Chris. *Rocks and Minerals*, New York: DK Publishing, 1992.

Raymo, Chet and Maureen E. *Written in Stone, A Geological History of the Northeastern United States*, Old Saybrook, Conn: Globe Pequot Press, 1989.

Mammals, reptiles, and amphibians

Godin, Alfred J. *Wild Mammals of New England*, Baltimore: Johns Hopkins Press, 1977.

Lazell, James D., Jr. *This Broken Archipelago*, New York: Quadrangle/The New York Times Book Company, 1976.

Regional and state guides

Steele, Frederic L. *At Timberline, A Nature Guide to the Mountains of the Northeast*, Boston: Appalachian Mountain Club, 1982.

Alden, Peter et al. *National Audubon Society Field Guide to New England*, New York: Alfred A. Knopf, 1998.

Leahy, Christopher, John Hanson Mitchell, and Thomas Conuel. *The Nature of Massachusetts*, New York: Addison-Wesley, 1996.

Sterling, Dorothy. *The Outer Lands, A Natural History Guide to Cape Cod, Martha's Vineyard, Nantucket, Block Island and Long Island*, New York: W. W. Norton, 1978.

Berril, Michael and Deborah. *A Sierra Club Naturalist's Guide, The North Atlantic Coast*, San Francisco: Sierra Club Books, 1981.

Jorgenson, Neil. *A Sierra Club Naturalist's Guide, Southern New England*, San Francisco: Sierra Club Books, 1978.

GLOSSARY

Accidental   A bird species seen only rarely in a certain region and whose normal territory is elsewhere. *See also* occasional.

Acre-foot   The amount of water required to cover one acre one foot deep.

Alkali sink   An alkaline habitat at the bottom of a basin where there is moisture under the surface.

Alluvial   Clay, sand, silt, pebbles, and rocks deposited by running water. River floodplains have alluvial deposits, sometimes called alluvial fans, where a stream exits from mountains onto flatland.

Aquifer   Underground layer of porous water-bearing sand, rock, or gravel.

Arthropod   Invertebrates, including insects, crustaceans, arachnids, and myriapods, with a semitransparent exoskeleton (hard outer structure) and a segmented body, with jointed appendages in articulated pairs.

ATV   All-terrain-vehicle. *See also* 4WD *and* ORV.

Barrier island   Coastal island produced by wave action and made of sand. Over time the island shifts and changes shape. Barrier islands protect the mainland from storms, tides, and winds.

Basking   The habit of certain creatures such as turtles, snakes, or alligators to expose themselves to the pleasant warmth of the sun by resting on logs, rocks, or other relatively dry areas.

Biome   A major ecological community such as a marsh or a forest.

Blowout   A hollow formed by wind erosion in a preexisting sand dune, often due to vegetation loss.

Bog   Wet, spongy ground filled with sphagnum moss and having highly acidic water.

Bottomland   Low-elevation alluvial area, close by a river. Sometimes also called "bottoms."

Brackish   Water that is less salty than sea water; often found in salt marshes, mangrove swamps, estuaries, and lagoons.

Breachway   A gap in a barrier beach or island, forming a connection between sea and lagoon.

Bushwhack   To hike through territory without established trails.

Cambium   In woody plants, a sheath of cells between external bark and internal wood that generates parallel rows of cells to make new tissue, either as secondary growth or cork.

Canopy   The highest layer of the forest, consisting of the crowns of the trees.

Carnivore   An animal that is primarily flesh eating. *See also* herbivore *and* omnivore.

Climax   In a stable ecological community, the plants and animals that will successfully continue to live there.

Colonial birds   Birds that live in relatively stable colonies, used annually for breeding and nesting.

Competition   A social behavior that organizes the sharing of resources such as space, food, and breeding partners when resources are in short supply.

Coniferous   Trees that are needle-leaved or scale-leaved; mostly evergreen and cone bearing, such as pines, spruces, and firs. *See also* deciduous.

Cordgrass   Grasses found in marshy areas, capable of growing in brackish waters. Varieties include salt-marsh cordgrass, hay, spike grass, and glasswort.

Crust   The outer layer of the earth, between 15 and 40 miles thick.

Crustacean   A hard-shelled, usually aquatic, arthropod such as a lobster or crab. *See also* arthropod.

DDT   An insecticide ($Cl_4H_9C_{l5}$), toxic to animals and human beings whether ingested or absorbed through skin; particularly devastating to certain bird populations, DDT was generally banned in the U.S. in 1972.

Deciduous   Plants that shed or lose their foliage at the conclusion of the growing season, as in "deciduous trees," such as hardwoods (maple, beech, oak, etc.). *See also* coniferous.

Delta   A triangular alluvial deposit at a river's mouth or at the mouth of a tidal inlet. *See also* alluvial.

Dominant   The species most characteristic of a plant or animal community, usually influencing the types and numbers of other species in the same community.

Ecological niche   An organism's function, status, or occupied area in its ecological community.

Ecosystem   A mostly self-contained community consisting of an environment and the animals and plants that live there.

Emergent plants   Plants adapted to living in shallow water or in saturated soils such as marshes or wetlands.

Endangered species   A species determined by the federal government to be in danger of extinction throughout all or a significant portion of its range (Endangered Species Act. 1973). *See also* threatened species.

Endemic species   Species that evolved in a certain place and live naturally nowhere else. *See also* indigenous species.

Epiphyte   A type of plant (often found in swamps) that lives on a tree instead of on the soil. Epiphytes are not parasitic; they collect their own water and minerals and perform photosynthesis.

Esker   An extended gravel ridge left by a river or stream that runs beneath a decaying glacier.

Estuary   The lower part of a river where freshwater meets tidal salt water. Usually characterized by abundant animal and plant life.

Evergreen   A tree, shrub, or other plant whose leaves remain green through all seasons.

Exotic   A plant or animal not native to the territory. Many exotic plants and animals displace native species.

Extirpation   The elimination of a species by unnatural causes, such as overhunting or fishing.

Fall line   A line between the piedmont and the coastal plain below which rivers flow through relatively flat terrain. Large rivers are navigable from the ocean to the fall line.

Fauna   Animals, especially those of a certain region or era, generally considered as a group. *See also* flora.

Fledge   Of young birds until they have their feathers and are able to fly.

Floodplain   A low-lying, flat area along a river where flooding is common.

Flora   Plants, especially those of a certain region or era, generally considered as a group. *See also* fauna.

Flyway   A migratory route, providing food and shelter, followed by large numbers of birds.

Forb   Any herb that is not in the grass family; forbs are commonly found in fields, prairies, or meadows.

4WD   Four-wheel-drive vehicle. *See also* ATV.

Frond   A fern leaf, a compound palm leaf, or a leaflike thallus (where leaf and stem are continuous), as with seaweed and lichen.

Glacial outwash   Sediment dropped by rivers or streams as they flow away from melting glaciers.

Glacial till   An unsorted mix of clay, sand, and rock transported and left by glacial action.

Gneiss   A common and rather erosion-resistant metamorphic rock originating from shale, characterized by alternating dark and light bands.

Grassy bald   A summit area devoid of trees due to shallow or absent soil overlying bedrock (ledge).

Greentree reservoir   An area seasonally flooded by opening dikes. Oaks, hickories, and other water-tolerant trees drop nuts (mast) into the water. Migratory waterfowl and other wildlife feed on the mast during winter.

Habitat   The area or environment where a plant or animal, or communities of plants or animals, normally live, as in "an alpine habitat."

Hammock   A fertile spot of high ground in a wetland that supports the growth of hardwood trees.

Hardwoods   Flowering trees such as oaks, hickories, maples, and others, as opposed to softwoods and coniferous trees such as pines and hemlocks.

Herbivore   An animal that feeds on plant life. *See also* carnivore *and* omnivore.

Heronry   Nesting and breeding site for herons.

Herptiles   The class of animals including reptiles and amphibians.

Holdfast   The attachment, in lieu of roots, that enables seaweed to grip a substrate such as a rock.

Hot spot   An opening in the earth's interior from which molten rock erupts, eventually forming a volcano.

Humus   Decomposed leaves and other organic material found, for instance, on the forest floor.

Impoundment   A man-made body of water controlled by dikes or levees.

Indigenous species   Species that arrived unaided by humans but that may also live in other locations.

Inholding   Private land surrounded by federal or state lands such as a wildlife refuge.

Intertidal zone   The beach or shoreline area located between low- and high-tide lines.

Introduced species   Species brought to a location by humans, intentionally or accidentally; also called nonnative or alien species. *See also* exotic.

Lichen   A ground-hugging plant, usually found on rocks, produced by an association between an alga, which manufactures food, and a fungus, which provides support.

Loess   Deep, fertile, and loamy soil deposited by wind, the deepest deposits reaching 200 feet.

Magma   Underground molten rock.

Management area   A section of land within a federal wildlife preserve or forest where specific wildlife management practices are implemented and studied.

Marsh   A low-elevation transitional area between water (the sea) and land, dominated by grasses in soft, wet soils.

Mast   A general word for nuts, acorns, and other food for wildlife produced by trees in autumn.

Meander   A winding stream, river, or path.

Mesozoic   A geologic era, 230–265 million years ago, during which dinosaurs appeared and became extinct, and birds and flowering plants first appeared.

Midden   An accumulation of organic material near a village or dwelling; also called a shell mound.

Migrant   An animal that moves from one habitat to another, as opposed to resident species that live permanently in the same habitat.

Mitigation   The act of creating or enlarging refuges or awarding them water rights to replace wildlife habitat lost because of the damming or channelization of rivers or the building of roads.

Moist-soil unit   A wet area that sprouts annual plants, which attract waterfowl. Naturally produced by river flooding, moist-soil units are artificially created through controlled watering.

Moraine   A formation of rock and soil debris transported and dropped by a glacier.

Neotropical   New World tropics, generally referring to central and northern South America.

Nesting species   Birds that take up permanent residence in a habitat.

Occasional   A bird species seen only occasionally in a certain region and whose normal territory is elsewhere. *See also* accidental.

Oceanic trench   The place where a sinking tectonic plate bends down, creating a declivity in the ocean floor.

Old field   A field that was once cultivated for crops but has been left to grow back into forest.

Old-growth forest   A forest characterized by large trees and a stable ecosystem. Old-growth forests are similar to pre-Colonial forests.

Omnivore   An animal that feeds on both plant and animal material. *See also* carnivore *and* herbivore.

ORVs   Off-road-vehicles. *See also* 4WD *and* ATV.

Oxbow   A curved section of water, once a bend in a river that was severed from the river when the river changed course. An oxbow lake is formed by the changing course of a river as it meanders through its floodplain.

Passerine   A bird in the *Passeriformes* order, primarily composed of perching birds and songbirds.

Peat   An accumulation of sphagnum moss and other organic material in wetland areas, known as peat bogs.

Petroglyph   Carving or inscription on a rock.

Photosynthesis   The process by which green plants use the energy in sunlight to create carbohydrates from carbon dioxide and water, generally releasing oxygen as a by-product.

Pictograph   Pictures painted on rock by indigenous peoples.

Pit and mound topography   Terrain characteristic of damp hemlock woods where shallow-rooted fallen trees create pits (former locations of trees) and mounds (upended root balls).

Plant community   Plants and animals that interact in a similar environment within a region.

Pleistocene   A geologic era, 10,000 to 1.8 million years ago, known as the great age of glaciers.

Prairie   An expansive, undulating, or flat grassland, usually without trees, generally on the plains of midcontinent North America. In the southeast, "prairie" refers to wet grasslands with standing water much of the year.

Prescribed burn   A fire that is intentionally set to reduce the buildup of dry organic matter in a forest or grassland to prevent catastrophic fires later on or to assist plant species whose seeds need intense heat to open.

Proclamation area   An area of open water beside or around a coastal refuge where waterfowl are protected from hunting.

Rain shadow   An area sheltered from heavy rainfall by mountains that, at their higher altitudes, have drawn much of the rain from the atmosphere.

Raptor   A bird of prey with a sharp curved beak and hooked talons. Raptors include hawks, eagles, owls, falcons, and ospreys.

Rhizome   A horizontal plant stem, often thick with reserved food material, from which grow shoots above and roots below.

Riparian   The bank and associated plant-life zone of any water body, including tidewaters.

Riverine   Living or located on the banks of a river.

Rookery   A nesting place for a colony of birds or other animals (seals, penguins, others).

Salt marsh   An expanse of tall grass, usually cordgrass and sedges, located in sheltered places such as the land side of coastal barrier islands or along river mouths and deltas at the sea.

Salt pan   A shallow pool of saline water formed by tidal action that usually provides abundant food for plovers, sandpipers, and other wading birds.

Scat   Animal fecal droppings.

Scrub   A dry area of sandy or otherwise poor soil that supports species adapted to such conditions, such as sand myrtle and prickly pear cactus, or dwarf forms of other species, such as oaks and palmettos.

Sea stack   A small, steep-sided rock island lying off the coast.

Second growth   Trees in a forest that grow naturally after the original stand is cut or burned. *See also* old-growth forest.

Seeps   Small springs that may dry up periodically.

Shorebird   A bird, such as a plover or sandpiper, frequently found on or near the seashore.

Shrub-steppe   Desertlike lands dominated by sagebrush, tumbleweed, and other dry-weather adapted plants.

Slough   A backwater or creek in a marshy area; sloughs sometimes dry into deep mud.

Spit   A narrow point of land, often of sand or gravel, extending into the water.

Staging area   A place where birds rest, gather strength, and prepare for the next stage of a journey.

Successional   Referring to a series of different plants that establish themselves by territories, from water's edge to drier ground. Also, the series of differing plants that reestablish themselves over time after a fire or the retreat of a glacier.

Sump   A pit or reservoir used as a drain or receptacle for liquids.

Swale   A low-lying, wet area of land.

Swamp   A spongy wetland supporting trees and shrubs (as opposed to a marsh, which is characterized by grasses). Swamps provide habitat for birds, turtles, alligators, and bears and serve as refuges for species extirpated elsewhere. *See also* extirpation.

Test   The hard, round exoskeleton of a sea urchin.

Threatened species   A species of plant or animal in which population numbers are declining, but not in immediate danger of extinction. Threatened species are protected under the Endangered Species Act of 1973. *See also* endangered species.

Tuber   A short, underground stem with buds from which new shoots grow.

Understory   Plants growing under the canopy of a forest. *See also* canopy.

Vascular plant   A fern or another seed-bearing plant with a series of channels for conveying nutrients.

Vernal pool   Shallow ponds that fill with spring ("vernal") rains or snowmelt and dry up as summer approaches; temporary homes to certain amphibians.

Wader   A long-legged bird, such as a crane or stork, usually found feeding in shallow water.

Wetland   A low moist area, often a marsh or swamp, especially in the context of its being the natural habitat of wildlife.

Wilderness Area   An area of land (within a national forest, national park, or a national wildlife refuge) protected under the 1964 Federal Wilderness Act. Logging, construction, and use of mechanized vehicles or tools are prohibited here and habitats are left in their pristine states. "Designated Wilderness" is the highest form of federal land protection.

Wrack line   Plant, animal, and unnatural debris left on the upper beach by a receding tide.

PHOTOGRAPHY CREDITS

We would like to thank the U. S. Fish & Wildlife Service for permission to publish photos from their collection, as well as the other contributing photographers for their wonderful imagery. The pages on which the photos appear are listed after each contributor.

Daniel B. Gibson pp. 3, 5

John & Karen Hollingsworth pp. ii–iii, 4, 6, 25, 40, 47, 54, 60, 62, 64, 80, 85, 101, 100, 135

Gary Kramer pp. xii, 7, 8, 17, 27, 36, 45, 51, 78, 86, 102, 109, 119, 127, 132, 138, 140

Christyna M. Laubach pp. 28, 38

René Laubach pp. 21, 22–23, 30, 33, 39, 57, 72, 88, 91, 105, 110, 112, 115, 120, 122, 128

U.S. Fish & Wildlife Service pp. 14, 53, 69, 97

ACKNOWLEDGMENTS

First and foremost I wish to thank Series Editor David Emblidge for conceiving the idea for this book and series, and for not letting the project die despite several false starts. He was a pleasure to work with. A well-deserved thank-you also to Don Young, who edited this volume with a fine-tooth comb and improved the manuscript markedly; he and I are detail-oriented kindred spirits.

The staff at Balliett & Fitzgerald, Inc., especially Editor Alexis Lipsitz, Design Director Sue Canavan, and Photo Editor Maria Fernandez, all played crucial roles in the production of this book. Likewise did the sponsors of the series, the National Audubon Society, who used their broad understanding of conservation issues to bolster the work.

This book could not have been produced without the cooperation of many dedicated U.S. Fish & Wildlife Service employees who answered queries and reviewed manuscripts. They are as follows: (Connecticut) Stewart B. McKinney NWR, William J. Kolodnicki; (Maine) Moosehorn NWR, Bob Peyton; Petit Manan NWR, Stan A. Skutek; Rachel Carson NWR, Susan Bloomfield; Sunkhaze Meadows NWR, Lauri S. Monroe; (Massachusetts) Great Meadows, Nantucket, and Oxbow NWRs, Manuel (Bud) Oliveira and Pamela Hess; Monomoy NWR, Sharon Ware; Parker River NWR, John L. Fillio and Steve Haydock; Silvio O. Conte NWR, Carolyn Boardman and Beth Goettel; (New Hampshire) Wapack NWR, Manuel (Bud) Oliveira; (Rhode Island) Block Island, Ninigret, Sachuest Point, and Trustom Pond NWRs, Charles Hebert; (Vermont) Missisquoi NWR, Robert A. Zelley. Thanks as well to Spence Conley, Director of Public Affairs for USF&WS Region 1, for supporting this project. Richard Bellevue of The Trustees of Reservations also reviewed the manuscript for Nantucket NWR.

A number of colleagues at Massachusetts Audubon acted as guides and mentors during my travels to particular properties that they know well. Among them are Bob Prescott of Wellfleet Bay Wildlife Sanctuary, and Don Reid (currently with The Trustees of Reservations) who taught me about Monomoy NWR. Others who added greatly to my knowledge base are: Christopher Leahy, Wayne Petersen, Jackie Sones, and Thomas F. Tyning.

Finally, but not lastly, my sincere appreciation goes to my wife of 25 years, Christyna, for serving as an able "field assistant," as she puts it, and for making those many hours we spent at New England's wildlife refuges even more enjoyable. Simon Geary, a dear British friend, accompanied Chris and me on many of our exploratory forays to these wonderful properties and added much with his keen eyesight and easy wit.

—René Laubach

ABOUT THE AUTHOR

René Laubach is Director, Massachusetts Audubon Society, Berkshire Sanctuaries, Lenox, Massachusetts. He is the author of *A Guide to Natural Places in the Berkshires* and of several nature-walks books for the New England region.

NATIONAL AUDUBON SOCIETY
Mission Statement

The mission of National Audubon Society, founded in 1905, is to conserve and restore natural ecosystems, focusing on birds, other wildlife, and their habitats for the benefit of humanity and the earth's biological diversity.

One of the largest, most effective environmental organizations, Audubon has more than 560,000 members, numerous state offices and nature centers, and 500+ chapters in the United States and Latin America, plus a professional staff of scientists, lobbyists, lawyers, policy analysts, and educators. Through our nationwide sanctuary system we manage 150,000 acres of critical wildlife habitat and unique natural areas for birds, wild animals, and rare plant life.

Our award-winning *Audubon* magazine, published six times a year and sent to all members, carries outstanding articles and color photography on wildlife and nature, and presents in-depth reports on critical environmental issues, as well as conservation news and commentary. We also publish *Field Notes*, a journal reporting on seasonal bird sightings continent-wide, and *Audubon Adventures*, a bimonthly children's newsletter reaching 500,000 students. Through our ecology camps and workshops in Maine, Connecticut, and Wyoming, we offer professional development for educators and activists; through Audubon Expedition Institute in Belfast, Maine, we offer unique, traveling undergraduate and graduate degree programs in Environmental Education.

Our acclaimed *World of Audubon* television documentaries on TBS deal with a variety of environmental themes, and our children's series for the Disney Channel, *Audubon's Animal Adventures*, introduces family audiences to endangered wildlife species. Other Audubon film and television projects include conservation-oriented movies, electronic field trips, and educational videos. National Audubon Society also sponsors books and interactive programs on nature, plus travel programs to exotic places like Antarctica, Africa, Australia, Baja California, Galapagos Islands, Indonesia, and Patagonia.

For information about how you can become an Audubon member, subscribe to Audubon Adventures, or learn more about our camps and workshops, please write or call:

National Audubon Society
Membership Dept.
700 Broadway
New York, New York 10003
212/979-3000
http://www.audubon.org

JOIN THE NATIONAL AUDUBON SOCIETY—RISK FREE!

Please send me my first issue of AUDUBON magazine and enroll me as a temporary member of the National Audubon Society at the $20 introductory rate—$15 off the regular rate. If I wish to continue as a member, I'll pay your bill when it arrives. If not, I'll return it marked "cancel," owe nothing, and keep the first issue free.

____ Payment Enclosed   ____ Bill Me

Name _____   _____

Street _____

City _____

State/zip _____

Please make checks payable to the National Audubon Society. Allow 4–6 weeks for delivery of magazine. $10 of dues is for AUDUBON magazine. Basic membership, dues are $35.

Mail to:

        NATIONAL AUDUBON SOCIETY
        Membership Data Center
        PO Box 52529
        Boulder, CO 80322-2529